The Politics of Order in Informal Markets

Property rights are important for economic exchange, but many governments don't protect them. Private market organizations can fill this gap by providing an institutional structure to enforce agreements, but with this power comes the ability to extort group members. Under what circumstances, then, will private organizations provide a stable environment for economic activity? Based on market case studies and a representative survey of traders in Lagos, Nigeria, this book argues that threats from the government can force an association to behave in ways that promote trade. The findings challenge the conventional wisdom that private good governance in developing countries thrives when the government keeps its hands off private group affairs. Instead, the author argues, leaders among traders behave in ways that promote trade primarily because of the threat of government intrusion.

Shelby Grossman is a Research Scholar at the Stanford Internet Observatory. She holds a Ph.D. in Government from Harvard University.

Cambridge Studies in Economics, Choice, and Society

Founding Editors

Timur Kuran, Duke University
Peter J. Boettke, George Mason University

This interdisciplinary series promotes original theoretical and empirical research as well as integrative syntheses involving links between individual choice, institutions, and social outcomes. Contributions are welcome from across the social sciences, particularly in the areas where economic analysis is joined with other disciplines such as comparative political economy, new institutional economics, and behavioral economics.

Books in the Series:

The Politics of Order in Informal Markets

How the State Shapes Private Governance

SHELBY GROSSMAN
Stanford University, California

CAMBRIDGE
UNIVERSITY PRESS

CAMBRIDGE
UNIVERSITY PRESS

Shaftesbury Road, Cambridge CB2 8EA, United Kingdom

One Liberty Plaza, 20th Floor, New York, NY 10006, USA

477 Williamstown Road, Port Melbourne, VIC 3207, Australia

314–321, 3rd Floor, Plot 3, Splendor Forum, Jasola District Centre, New Delhi – 110025, India

103 Penang Road, #05–06/07, Visioncrest Commercial, Singapore 238467

Cambridge University Press is part of Cambridge University Press & Assessment, a department of the University of Cambridge.

We share the University's mission to contribute to society through the pursuit of education, learning and research at the highest international levels of excellence.

www.cambridge.org
Information on this title: www.cambridge.org/9781108984713

DOI: 10.1017/9781108984980

© Cambridge University Press & Assessment 2021

First published 2021
First paperback edition 2022

A catalogue record for this publication is available from the British Library

Library of Congress Cataloging-in-Publication data
NAMES: Grossman, Shelby, author.
TITLE: The politics of order in informal markets : how the state shapes
    private governance / Shelby Grossman, Stanford University, California.
DESCRIPTION: 1 Edition. | New York : Cambridge University Press, 2021. |
    Series: Cambridge studies in economics, choice, and society | Includes
    bibliographical references and index.
IDENTIFIERS: LCCN 2021014522 | ISBN 9781108833493 (hardback) | ISBN
    9781108984713 (paperback) | ISBN 9781108984980 (ebook)
SUBJECTS: LCSH: Informal sector (Economics) – Developing countries. |
    Private companies – Developing countries. | Business and
    politics – Developing countries. | Economic policy – Developing countries.
    | BISAC: POLITICAL SCIENCE / Public Policy / Economic Policy | POLITICAL
    SCIENCE / Public Policy / Economic Policy
CLASSIFICATION: LCC HD2346.5 .G76 2021 | DDC 381–dc23
LC record available at https://lccn.loc.gov/2021014522

ISBN   978-1-108-83349-3   Hardback
ISBN   978-1-108-98471-3   Paperback

Contents

Figures

Tables

Preface

Property rights are important for economic exchange, but in many parts of the world they are not publicly guaranteed. Private market associations can fill this gap by providing an institutional structure to enforce agreements, but with this power comes the ability to extort from group members. Under what circumstances do private associations provide a stable environment for economic activity? I examine original survey data collected from 1,179 randomly sampled traders across 199 markets in Lagos, Nigeria. I combine these results with market case studies and find that markets maintain institutions to support trade not in the *absence* of government, but rather in *response to* active government interference. I argue that associations develop pro-trade institutions when threatened by politicians they perceive to be predatory, and when the organization can respond with threats of its own; the latter is easier when traders are not competing with one another. In order to maintain this balance of power, the association will not extort because it needs trader support to maintain the credibility of its threats to mobilize against predatory politicians.

Acknowledgments

In the summer of 2010 I was feeling sad that my original dissertation idea was not panning out. I wanted to study how Lebanese trading communities organized themselves in Nigeria, but struggled to get Lebanese businesspeople to agree to be interviewed. At the end of the summer, I visited Lagos for the first time and had the chance to wander around the markets. Nigerian traders – though often quite secretive as well – turned out to be more forthcoming than the Lebanese traders. I realized I could study trader organization with a different population.

I am grateful to all of the traders who spoke with me for this project. For very good reasons they are often loath to discuss both details about their business and politics, but so many traders chose to trust me. Listening to their stories about market politics and learning how savvy they were in managing their businesses kept me going throughout a year of otherwise lonely fieldwork. There were days when Lagos felt so overwhelming that I was tempted to not even leave my apartment. But if I succeeded in having just one conversation with a trader, I came home feeling like I had gained great insight into the world and couldn't imagine having spent the day doing anything else. In particular, I thank Edwin Nnamdi Onye and Alhaja Marsha, along with two traders from Ladipo Spare Parts Market, and a former market manager in Lekki. I hope they all feel that this book captures something approximating the realities of market governance in Lagos. I also so appreciate the many local and state government officials who spoke with me for this book.

Thanks to my dissertation committee. To Robert Bates: you listened to my interests and helped me find an intellectual home for them. Early on you pointed me to key readings that shaped the way I think about organizational behavior and provided thoughtful advice after each fieldwork trip about how to proceed. With thoughtful honesty, you pointed out ways I could improve as a scholar throughout my time in graduate school. This type of feedback is hard to come by, and I was always grateful for it.

I still cannot believe I found my way to Catherine Duggan, whose research interests were so closely aligned with my own. Catherine, I loved nerding out with you about the intricacies of everything from in-group policing to traders' transaction decisions. To Jeffry Frieden: it is a cliché to thank you for feedback on theory, but that is what I must do here. You forced me to think through the logic of every assertion I made, and were a positive, encouraging, and accessible advisor. And I'm grateful to James Robinson for helping me find a second intellectual home with the Centre for Economic and Policy Research's community of scholars. You pushed me to think through the political dimensions of trade and were always so confident that there *was* an important political dimension to be uncovered. To all the members of my committee: the excitement you conveyed in meetings about my findings motivated me in my research.

To my dissertation reading group – Jen Pan, Amanda Pinkston, Molly Roberts, Chiara Superti, and Vanessa Williamson – our group was exactly what I imagined graduate school would be. We had such intellectual and supportive discussions, and certainly no one has engaged as much with this project as all of you. You each gave me important feedback at every step of this project. As importantly, I learned so much from following the development of your projects.

Amanda, our seven years in graduate school were a happy and intellectually exciting time of my life because of you. We became friends on our first day and submitted our dissertations on the same day. If you wanted to take three more years to graduate, I would have as well, just to be around you. If you wanted to be done in five, I would have figured out a way to hustle, as the prospect of graduate school without you was inconceivable. Fieldwork is so hard, and if you hadn't been around to enthusiastically listen to my stories, I don't know what I would have done. I am so grateful for your friendship.

Many people gave me helpful feedback on this project during and after graduate school. Thank you to Mai Hassan, Steven Levitsky, Noah Nathan, Jonathan Phillips, and Tristan Reed. Graeme Blair: thanks for introducing me to Lagos and for making sure my framework for this project was always compelling, clear, and polished. Gwyneth McClendon, you gave me thoughtful feedback on my work and answered a variety of professionalization questions over the years without ever making me feel bad for asking. To Jonathan Phillips, your consistently detailed and constructive feedback was incredibly helpful. Diane de Gramont, thanks for sharing important insights about Lagos politics. I'm grateful to the participants at many workshops, including Harvard's Comparative Politics workshop; Stanford's Africa Table; George Mason's Workshop in Philosophy, Politics, and Economics; Duke's Political Institutions workshop; and the Centre for the Study of Governance and Society's seminar at King's College London.

After graduate school I did a postdoctoral fellowship at Stanford's Center on Democracy, Development, and the Rule of Law. I am grateful to Frank Fukuyama and Stephen Stedman for this year of uninterrupted time to expand on my dissertation work and for financially supporting an invaluable book workshop. To my book workshop participants – Leo Arriola, Adam Auerbach, Karen Feree, Didi Kuo, Dan Mattingly, and Alison Post – you took the time to carefully read a far inferior version of this manuscript and made it better.

Thanks go especially to Didi, whose trajectory I have followed since 2004. I look forward to seeing what you do next so I know what is in store for my future. Lauren Young: you were such a fun and kind officemate for our post-doc year. I'm glad we got to spend so much time together.

Lagos and Cambridge are expensive, and I am grateful to all of the organizations that financially supported this research. Thanks go to Chris Woodruff and the Private Enterprise Development in Low-Income Countries (PEDL) initiative for funding my work as an early graduate student and welcoming me, as a political scientist, into the PEDL community. The research was also made possible by support from the Weatherhead Center for International Affairs, the International Growth Centre, the Templeton Foundation, the Foreign Language and Area Study Program, the Hartley R. Rogers Graduate Student Dissertation Fellowship, and the Samuel P. Huntington Doctoral Dissertation Fellowship.

I spent two years at the University of Memphis, and I'm grateful for support from the political science community there. Mike Sances, your time helping me make an article version of a chapter in this book stronger in turn strengthened the book as a whole. And thanks go to Matthias Kaelberer for supporting me in many ways to finish up the last bits of research for this project.

The undergraduate political science honors program at Emory University got me excited about political science research. I thank Rick Donor and Beth Reingold for structuring this program so thoughtfully and giving me the chance to travel to Liberia for my undergraduate thesis. Interning at The Carter Center and working for Ashley Barr in college changed my life. Ashley, you got me excited about African politics, modeled strong leadership, and gave me frequent and constructive feedback.

I am thrilled this project found its home with the Economics, Choice, and Society series at Cambridge University Press. There is no better fit. I thank the series editors, Pete Boettke and Timur Kuran, for your feedback and guidance, and to the three reviewers whose suggestions greatly improved the project. David Skarbek, the project would not have found this series without you. Thank you for mentoring me throughout the book publishing process. To Kimberly Friel, my writing editor: your edits helped me feel more confident in this final product. The final months of revisions took place at the Redwood City Public Library with Jessie Sebor. Thanks, Jessie, for your friendship and fro-yo walks. You helped me get this to the finish line.

I have so much appreciation for the Lagos Trader Project team. First, Meredith Startz, you taught me how to do survey work, and I have learned so much from you about what it means to be a careful researcher. Working with you has made everything about research more enjoyable. Cooking curry on a hot plate on the floor of a mediocre hotel room could be miserable, but doing it with you made it a funny story. I feel lucky to have worked with Hakeem Bishi, Yemi Ogundare, Sam Adesanya, and Seun Odeyemi, the field management team, for more than four years. I am so proud of this research organization we have built together, and of its values. I'm grateful to every member of the Lagos Trader Project team – including our stellar enumerators and auditors – for the role you all have played in acquiring the data in this book. Thanks also go to Dylan Groves, Alex Ojo, and Nicole Wilson for the varied roles they played in supporting this project.

My family's invaluable support helped lead to this book. To my parents, you encouraged me to go to Liberia on my own in college and provided support at so many critical junctures. Thanks for calling my bank every time my debit card was copied in Nigeria, for much needed airport pick-ups after fieldwork trips, and for helping me move at least six times. Jeffrey, thanks for paying my cell phone bill during graduate school (and, uh, still). Thanks to Arta Khakpour for thinking this project was interesting and helping me become more sophisticated in the way I think about politics. Finishing this project was enjoyable because of your and Cabbage's companionship.

Introduction

Public institutions rarely serve the needs of informal workers, who encompass as much as 62 percent of global employment (Kok and Berrios, 2019). For instance, informal entrepreneurs often view courts as biased, inefficient, and unequipped to regulate off-the-books transactions, so they do not rely on them for protection. Instead, they must bear the full cost of swindles or errors themselves. The legal system would therefore be of little help to traders who stock up on what they thought were new smartphones, only to discover that they were refurbished and must be sold at a loss. A large body of work maintains that private associations can step in to fill this regulatory gap by enforcing contracts, but this is not always the case. Although informal traders frequently belong to such groups, not all of them promote trade. Indeed, many extort from traders in their own associations. Markets in Lagos, Nigeria, provide examples of both types of associations.

For example, two markets in the center of the city appear to be similar from the outside. Yet the markets are governed very differently. The first is a wine market with about 1,000 traders, and on the surface it looks similar to many other markets in the city. Small shops densely line narrow dirt paths. Shop owners, who might have one employee, sit on white plastic stools, waiting for customers. Like hundreds of other markets in the city, this one is governed by a private traders' association, which is headed by a trader who was elected to serve as the primary leader. Traders in the second market also sell products that are difficult to inspect at the point of sale, in this case cosmetics, food items, and some wine.

The wine market leader's administration is a model of good governance. The leader supports a wide variety of policies that promote trade. For example, the market leader impartially investigates customer complaints and confiscates wine that is substandard or falsely branded, and potentially fines the trader responsible. Similarly, if a supplier sells bad wine to a trader in his or her association, the trader informs the market leader. The market leader will investigate and may organize a market-wide boycott of that supplier.

By contrast, the leader of the second market extorts from his traders. He collects fees from them that he says will be used to pay ten security guards at a salary of $83/month, when in fact there are only four guards who are paid just $56/month. Similarly, traders report that they pay for waste collection, but the trash is collected only infrequently. "It is obvious [the market leader] doesn't [financially] settle the people who are supposed to carry out dirt in this market," one trader said. "I don't know what [he] is using the money for." If a supplier or customer wrongs a trader in this market, the leader does not intervene.

The underlying dynamics explaining divergent outcomes in these two markets are not obvious. The leaders of both markets are strong in the sense that they are able to control the market's internal affairs. For example, they both have the authority to lock up a trader's shop to sanction rule-breaking. Yet one uses this power to promote trade, such as by punishing traders who cheat, while the other uses it to extort from the traders. This book examines what motivates leaders to carry out trade-promoting policies. Specifically, I investigate the conditions under which market leaders share information about dubious suppliers and customers and impartially mediate disputes, versus when they will be unengaged or predate. I use the term "private governance" to mean the extent to which leaders provide these trade-promoting policies. "Good private governance" indicates that a leader provides many of these services.

A dominant strand of thought suggests that private institutions arise to fill the vacuum left by weak or absent states. These institutions are thought to thrive in the absence of political interference. According to this logic, private good governance thrives in the absence of meddling malevolent politicians. Therefore, the first market's trade-supportive environment should be a function of stereotypically corrupt politicians keeping their hands out of the market's affairs, while the second market's problems must emanate from public interference.

Yet I find that the opposite is true: the wine market faces extensive government intervention, and its leader maintains pro-trade services as a strategy to *respond* to threats of interference. He punishes the sale of substandard wine to reduce the likelihood that disagreements with customers will escalate to the attention of a regulatory agency that uses any dispute as an excuse to extract rents from the market. Unlike the second leader, the first market leader does not extort from traders because he needs their support in order to politically mobilize them to preempt local government extortion. The second market does not face threats from the regulatory agency, and the local government it falls under is far less intrusive. These cases are not the exception. Indeed, I will show that they are the rule: informal institutions perform *better* under the shadow of government, and *worse* in the absence of government interference.

The argument, in short, is that strong leaders – those who are able to control the internal affairs of their group and have the ability to enforce decisions within the group – can use their strength either to predate on group members or to promote trade. Strong leaders will be motivated to engage in the latter strategy when they face the prospect of government intrusion. Threats from the government motivate trade-promoting policies because (1) the leader needs to minimize group disputes to reduce the likelihood of state intervention, and (2) the leader needs the support of group members to mobilize against state threats. In short, strong leaders maintain sophisticated policies to support trade not in the *absence* of government, but rather in response to active government interference.

But the threat of politician intrusion does not always result in private good governance. When traders are in competition with one another, business will feel like a zero-sum game. Markets may be spaces of secrecy, with each man for himself. In these circumstances, market leaders will struggle to unify traders. As a result, I expect that threats of government meddling are more likely to lead to better private governance when traders are selling different products, and are not directly in competition with one another.

1.1 WHY THESE PRIVATE LEADERS MATTER

There are hundreds of other similar markets in Lagos, and virtually all are structured in the same way: they are in physically delimited spaces, governed by a handful of traders who were elected in popular market elections. Societal norms in much of the developing world are such that these market leaders are considered liaisons with government officials. They often exert control over access to shops in a market, even when shops are in privately owned structures. In a place like Lagos where up to 67 percent of residents report working in the informal economy,[1] market leadership matters.

And Lagos is not an exception. In Nigeria as a whole, and indeed in developing countries in general, 41 percent of GDP comes from the informal economy.[2] Moreover, the associational nature of trade is not unique to Nigeria (e.g., Cross, 1998; Hummel, 2017a). The world over, retailers, tailors, and shoe shiners are organized and operate under the jurisdiction of private leaders. Similar associations govern slums, informal transportation, and laborers.

For a trader in America, public institutions (in general) impartially enforce contracts and protect property rights. Police arrest suppliers who cheat, mitigating the need for acquiring information about opportunistic individuals. When the rule of law is weak – that is, when laws are unclear and agreements are unevenly and inefficiently enforced – the government cannot be relied upon for these services. This presents a huge barrier to trade. Policies like those the

---

[1] Author's analysis of the 2012 Lagos State Household Survey ($n = 10,000$). The question asked, "The daily activity of the [respondent] can be categorized into: 1) Formal sector (white collar job), 2) Informal sector (bricklaying, barbing, tailoring, vulcanizer, etc.)." This question likely results in overreporting of the informal sector work, as individuals can work in the formal sector but not consider themselves white-collar workers.

[2] The Nigeria estimate is from the Nigerian National Bureau of Statistics. "Formal and Informal Sector Split of Gross Domestic Product: 2015." 2016. http://nigerianstat.gov.ng/. The developing countries estimate is from Schneider (2005).

wine market leader enforces are critically important for informal traders, who I define as those with businesses that are not registered with all relevant government entities or who conduct transactions that are not formally documented. The wine market leader is doing essentially three things: not predating on his own traders (which includes respecting the validity of shop leases), impartially enforcing contracts, and collecting and sharing information about dishonest suppliers and customers so as to avoid trading with them. For a huge percentage of individuals around the world, whether trade thrives is largely a function of the private policies that govern the space in which trade is conducted.

Moreover, contract enforcement is especially important for capital-constrained traders, who must be able to buy their stock from suppliers on credit. Traders with unregistered businesses may be ineligible for bank loans. Even traders with registered businesses struggle to access bank financing: more than 25 percent of *registered* firms in sub-Saharan Africa report that access to finance is their main obstacle to growth (Beck and Cull, 2014). Indeed, in Africa as a whole, supplier credit finances virtually the same amount of working capital as bank loans (World Bank, 2007). Yet suppliers understand the high risk that traders may not be able to repay them and thus are discerning in deciding to whom to offer products on credit. When market leaders create conditions that encourage repayment – for example, by impartially mediating disputes about repayment – suppliers will feel more comfortable providing credit in that market association.

Likewise, to stay in business, traders often need to give products to customers on credit and assume the risk that they might not be repaid. Here again, market leader policies that encourage repayment – for example, banning a customer from a market until they have repaid – have a huge impact on traders' businesses. These institutions help traders feel secure when extending credit.

In rural contexts, family and social ties can increase cooperation. For example, a supplier may be willing to provide products on credit to a trader who goes to church with her uncle. Similarly, a trader may be willing to sell a phone charger on credit to a customer with children at the same school as hers. These social ties can motivate repayment. City markets, however, rely on one-off impersonal trade: traders do not expect to see each other in other settings. When leaders like the wine market head share information about dishonest suppliers and customers, they provide an immensely valuable service. They are enabling contractual trade that should help traders to grow their businesses.

Property rights protection is another valuable service private group leaders can offer (or not). In dense urban environments, access to land on which to sell products is an important asset. Many urban poor experience insecure property rights, which can make medium- and long-term business planning decisions difficult. The wine market leader respects shop leases and accounts properly for the fees received from traders. In contrast, the other market leader discussed earlier misappropriates fees, and some predatory market leaders will occasionally kick a trader out of a shop before their lease ends. In short, when private market institutions work effectively, they can dramatically improve economic conditions in the informal sector.

1.2 THE ARGUMENT: HOW THREATS OF STATE INTERFERENCE SUSTAIN PRIVATE PRO-TRADE POLICIES

Threats of state interference, I propose, motivate strong group leaders to invest in and sustain policies that will promote trade within the group, particularly when group members are not directly competing with one another. I use the terms "group" and "organization" interchangeably. The group under study in this book is the market association, but the argument could apply to other types of business or resident associations. For simplicity, I conceptualize groups as having a single leader, although many groups are governed by a team of individuals. In the markets studied here, groups might have multiple leaders, but power is typically concentrated in the hands of one person. To avoid confusion about whether "association" references a group or a leader, I avoid this term except in cases where its meaning is unambiguous.

A leader of a group (whether public or private) who is strong enough to protect property rights and enforce contracts also has the power to confiscate the wealth of the members – what Barry Weingast calls "the fundamental political dilemma of an economic system" (1995, p. 1). A large, diverse, and interdisciplinary literature has described the characteristics that define successful self-governing organizations in the absence of impartial public institutions that protect property rights. However, this body of work rarely grapples with when, why, and how some groups succeed in developing these institutions, while others do not. I address this gap in the literature by exploring what motivates leaders to invest in pro-trade policies, when they *could* use their strength to predate.

The existence of pro-trade policies – particularly those related to information sharing and enforcement – is not a foregone conclusion, for a variety of reasons. A novel contribution of my argument is to highlight that such policies entail large short-term costs for a leader. First, what are these policies? Strong information-sharing institutions inform group members about the past behavior of potential trading partners to help them avoid entering into risky transactions with dishonest individuals. Enforcement mechanisms ensure the implementation of agreements, punish dishonest outsiders (through boycotts), and penalize opportunistic insiders through impartial and efficient in-group policing. A number of studies have described groups in which one or more of these institutions are present and support cooperation.[3]

Both types of pro-trade policies entail costs to the leaders, who must either motivate members to share information about people who have cheated them – a difficult endeavor when group members compete with each other and

---

3 See Greif (2006) for a discussion of a group with information sharing, Milgrom (1990) for a group with enforcement institutions, and Fearon and Laitin (1996) for groups with in-group policing.

individually have little incentive to share such information – or occasionally make rulings in disputes that go against the short-term interests of group members. Therefore, we will only observe these policies if the benefits to a group leader outweigh the costs. I am building on research by Barak Richman (2017) in theorizing about the role of within-group competition; many studies either claim that group members are not in fact competing with each other (Greif, 2006) or ignore the role of competition and focus only on what happens once collective problems have been overcome.

These costs highlight the importance of group leaders in large groups. Of course, it is possible to imagine these trade-supporting policies being sustained in the absence of leaders. Perhaps in some exceptional cases there are large groups of traders where norms of honesty are strong, social embeddedness induces reputable behavior, and truthful information about traders' reputations spreads quickly. But in general, I expect leaders to be critical, particularly in urban areas where social embeddedness cannot be assumed and there are incentives to keep secrets and spread lies.

While private groups are often viewed as substitutes for state regulations, the reality is far more complex. Groups and the state often coexist as political adversaries. The incentives created by this adversarial relationship determine how group leaders will govern.

My argument focuses on two actors: group leaders and public officials (such as local politicians, the police, and bureaucrats working for regulatory agencies). Traders (group members) play a lesser role in the theory. I assume that group leaders are self-interested and aim to maximize their income by maintaining their position, and thus their power to tax group members. Public officials' incentives vary – some local politicians may hope for higher office, which requires impressing patrons by showing what they can accomplish. Others might wish to avoid rocking the boat and plan to retire after their term. Police and regulatory officials will aim to keep their jobs, which could involve interfering more or less in the affairs of private groups, depending on their supervisors' incentives.

I argue that whether leaders need member support to keep meddling public officials at bay determines the degree to which leaders serve member interests. When public officials (such as politicians) lack a track record of acting in the public interest, groups will perceive the prospect of their intrusion as threatening and contrary to group interests. Where public officials try to interfere, leaders are more likely to support private trade-promoting policies. Under this umbrella concept, I focus on policies that reduce disputes (including information sharing and enforcement policies) and the avoidance of private extortion. A desire to fend off state threats can explain the presence of both. Leaders will work to reduce disputes to avoid them escalating to the attention of a potentially predatory government. Leaders will limit their extortion when they need to mobilize traders in order to collectively deter undesirable government behavior. I outline this logic in Figure 1.1.

What do threats of interference from public officials look like? These threats will vary by group type. In Lagos, local politicians might want to demolish

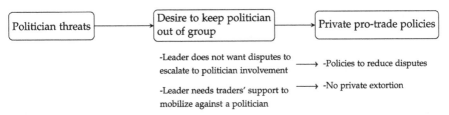

FIGURE 1.1 **How politician threats lead to private pro-trade policies.** The outcome of interest is private trade-promoting policies, including those that reduce disputes (including information sharing and enforcement policies) and private extortion. The presence of both can be explained by a desire to fend off politician threats. Leaders will work to reduce disputes to prevent them from escalating to the attention of a politician. Leaders will limit their extortion when they need to mobilize traders in order to collectively deter undesirable politician behavior

and renovate older markets. Traders are displaced during renovations and are often priced out of shops in the new market. Alternatively, local politicians may try to raise taxes. Regulatory agencies might threaten to lock shops in the market or enter the market with police who scare customers away. Markets on local government land are more vulnerable to these threats, as state officials have more rights to intervene and can collect a wider set of fees. Critically, these threats can vary within a city, and even within a local government. For idiosyncratic reasons, one market might be under threat of demolition, while a neighboring market might not.

Why will these threats limit private extortion? A strong leader wants to keep the government out of the group. The leader's threats against the government, however, are credible only if she can mobilize members to protest or vote as a bloc, or otherwise collectively sanction politicians (Bates and Lien, 1985). Such mobilization requires the sympathies of members. In efforts to maintain this support, the leader will be less likely to extort. This part of the argument has parallels to the state-building literature. For Charles Tilly (1992), a group leader's ability to resist an external threat requires support from group members, which incentivizes negotiation and exchange between the group leader and group members. According to Miguel Centeno (2003), external threats only promote institution building under certain conditions, which involve a certain level of organizational capacity.[4]

Consider the case of a market in the north of Lagos, which falls under a local government that has repeatedly tried to demolish it. The market

---

[4] My argument has parallels to Oliver Williamson's theory that two actors can provide each other with hostages to facilitate contractual trade (1983), and to arguments that a balance of power between the state and businesses can shape tax rates (Luong and Weinthal, 2004) and constrain corruption (Kang, 2002). There are also parallels to Catherine Duggan (Forthcoming), who argues that private lending markets grow when the state can check their power, primarily by preventing lenders from stealing from their clients. This leads potential borrowers to trust lenders. This argument also builds on work that suggests external threats, such as police repression, can motivate group solidarity (Thachil, 2015).

leader, in response, has mobilized traders against the local government. The association has successfully deterred four renovation attempts and brought the local government to court. In early 2018, the market leader appealed to the Lagos state governor, implicitly threatening the state party with the market's political strength: "We are begging [the governor] to wade into this matter," the market leaders told a reporter. "We know he is not the brain behind the alleged demolition as [the local government] claim[s]. We are all [ruling party] members and we want our governor to win a second term." The local government chairman, in turn, said that the governor "believes the market does not meet up with the megacity status," a common force that motivates local politicians to modernize their communities.[5] If the market leader had been extorting from traders, it is unlikely he would have been able to mobilize them to credibly protest and fend off the demolition.

Why would the threat of politician interference encourage a leader to facilitate information sharing? In short, the prospect of intrusion increases the gains to the leader of keeping her house in order. Disputes provide an opportunity for public officials to intervene, such as the police entering a market to deal with an altercation. If a leader permitted fraudulent behavior, such as allowing a trader to sell substandard products, public officials could exploit a customer complaint as an opportunity to intervene in the market and extract revenue. By policing member actions and eliciting and sharing information about outside swindlers, the leader limits disputes, and thus minimizes opportunities for government extortion, which can threaten the leader's influence. I expect government threats will have these consequences when the leader is strong.

Threats will not always lead to private good governance. I expect that, when group members compete with each other, it will be harder for leaders to elicit information about dishonest trading partners. It will also be harder to promote group cooperation of any sort, including protest efforts. I therefore expect high levels of intragroup competition to frustrate group leaders' efforts to support trade.

Could group leaders and state officials collude, throwing group members under the bus to advance elite interests? I expect such collusion to be uncommon, as the benefits to the group leader will only rarely outweigh the costs of maintaining a collusive arrangement. What we know about collusion in general suggests that it is sustained only when there are very sophisticated institutions to prevent one member of a colluding team from secretly defecting (Marshall and Marx, 2012). I expect these arrangements to be hard to support in low-trust environments. I expect collusion to be possible only when a group leader's autonomy is imminently threatened, and even then it should be rare.

---

[5] Erewuba, Paul. March 20, 2018. "Lagos traders send SOS to Ambode over planned market demolition." http://sunnewsonline.com/lagos-traders-send-sos-to-ambode-over-planned-market-demolition-2/

1.3 BROADER IMPLICATIONS

The evidence presented in this book has two main implications for our understanding of the role of politics in economic development. First, it suggests a channel for development that does not rely on a developmental state. Second, it updates our understanding of the factors that sustain private pro-trade policies in groups that extend beyond the informal sector.

1.3.1 A New Role for Politics in Economic Development

The notion of state–society struggles promoting trade is distinct from descriptions of partnerships between the state and societal groups that are seen in research on co-production (Mitlin, 2008; Ostrom, 1996) and on how developmental states are effective at promoting economic growth (Doner, 1992; Evans, 1995). Those who argue that under a very specific condition – when the state is developmental – close cooperation between the state and business associations is critical for growth tell us little about the conditions under which we would observe localized growth in non-developmental states.

I am, of course, not the first to argue that a balance of power between the state and society can lead to economic growth.[6] My contribution is to introduce two mechanisms through which this balance of power can shape private governance, shown earlier in Figure 1.1. In contrast to accounts of private governance that suggest private policies substitute for public policies (e.g., McMillan and Woodruff, 1999), I argue that, as the government attempts to intervene in private groups, private governance improves.

1.3.2 How Private Pro-Trade Policies Are Sustained

A vast interdisciplinary literature proposes that self-governance will emerge when it is needed, and focuses on describing the ways in which thriving groups function, but not on the conditions that make well-governed groups more or less likely. Robert Ellickson documents high levels of rancher cooperation in 1970s California, despite little knowledge of relevant legal provisions. "Order often arises spontaneously," Ellickson asserts (1991, p. 4). Edward Stringham has argued in his series of papers on private contract enforcement in early European stock exchanges (Stringham, 2003, 2002) that trader reputations simply become *known*; he does not explain *how* (e.g., Stringham, 2002, p. 17).

In considering the roots of the rule of law, Gillian Hadfield and Barry Weingast (2014) similarly focus on the role of decentralized collective punishment. While they do not assume that private good governance will emerge when needed, their expectation of what private good governance looks like does

---

[6] Karl Polanyi, for example, has proposed that untempered market liberalism presents enormous perils (1944). David Kang has argued that a balance of power between the state and businesses can constrain corruption (2002).

not explicitly consider the role of group leaders. My contribution is to high-light that – with the exception of small groups – empirically, the reputational institutions Hadfield and Weingast describe almost always require private lead-ers. Indeed, even groups with dense social networks, such as the New York Diamond Dealers Club which is comprised primarily of Orthodox Jews, have leaders who enforce policies that sustain cooperation (2001, 2017). When we acknowledge that groups have leaders, we must then ask what motivates these leaders to invest in policies that support trade rather than extort from their members.

I build on research that explores the political factors that make private good governance more likely. Elinor Ostrom (1990) suggests that the government can support private good governance by offsetting the costs of monitoring shared resource usage. Timothy Frye (2000) proposes that the government can lower the risk of information sharing within private groups by keeping tax rates low, as the consequences of a business sharing information with the gov-ernment about another business's volume of trade would be less severe in terms of tax penalties. My contribution in this book is to show that, even when the government is not offsetting the costs of group governance, politicians can still incentivize the creation of such policies.

In particular, I am introducing an argument for when we will see trade-promoting groups in cities, where traders may not be embedded in each other's lives, nor in the lives of their group leader. In the absence of social embedded-ness, traders will be less likely to cooperate with each other, and leaders will feel less socially constrained to act honestly. In so doing, I take up the call from urban politics scholars to consider the unique coordination challenges in cities where there is greater social diversity and population turnover (Auerbach et al., 2018).

1.4 ADDITIONAL FACTORS THAT MAY SHAPE PRIVATE GOOD GOVERNANCE

Why would a trader ever join a market with a predatory leader? And even if they made the mistake of joining a badly governed market, could they not compel the leader to behave better? Moreover, could a leader's time horizon determine how they govern? I now turn to these alternative explanations.

A potential criticism of the argument is that successful traders select into well-governed markets, and that this (rather than the balance of power argument) explains the persistence of different market governance equilibria. However, I expect that traders rarely sort in this way for two reasons. First, group membership is relatively sticky, making it difficult for individuals to frequently switch associational membership. The set of possible groups may be limited. For example, in Lagos, only two big markets sell used car spare parts. Likewise, one can imagine that a member of a badly governed union for hairstylists would not have many other unions to choose from. Second, outsiders have incomplete information about group conditions before join-ing. In competitive business environments, traders in a market will have no incentive to be truthful with potential new entrants about market leadership. These assumptions do not hold for all groups everywhere, but they do hold for many important groups, such as trade unions and business associations.

Should not the group members then be able to act collectively to overthrow predatory group leaders, or at least pressure them to refrain from extorting? The hurdles to such sanctioning are greater than assumed. Sanctioning is a long and costly process, and, in the meantime, leaders continue to predate. Traders hold little power over their leaders, particularly in cities where leaders are unlikely to be embedded in the social lives of traders.

If sanctioning is difficult, the obstacles to mutiny are enormous. Mutiny is, first and foremost, a collective action problem. Such problems are easier to overcome with leader guidance, but in cases of potential mutiny, the recognized leader is, by definition, not part of such collective efforts. Further, mutiny is exceptionally risky. Group members must trust that many of their peers will follow through on a promise to mutiny. But paradoxically, in groups where mutiny is desirable, a predatory leader could have cultivated distrust among group members. Group trust is especially challenging in urban markets where traders are unlikely to be socially embedded in each other's lives. While group sanctioning of a leader and mutiny are theoretically possible, these actions should be empirically rare in urban private groups.

Is a long time horizon sufficient to align the incentives between the leader and group members as Mancur Olson has theorized (2000)? After all, if group leaders aim to maximize their income, which is a function of fees they collect from group members proportional to the amount of wealth generated in the group, greater group order would seem to increase group-derived leader profits over the long term. Yet a long time horizon may not be sufficient to constrain short-term temptations to extort. Leaders can have conflicts of interest, such as other businesses and income streams, both inside and outside the market. These may encourage them to act on short-term opportunities at the expense of long-term group revenue growth (Ostrom, 1990). I directly consider these explanatory variables in my empirical analysis.

In short, I expect the role of sorting, sanctioning, and leader time horizon to have only a limited effect on the nature of private governance due to over-looked impediments, in particular obstacles to cooperation. In Chapter 4 I expand on these alternative explanations and introduce other theories related to group heterogeneity, competition and learning across markets, variation in public institutional quality, and the type of products sold in the market. In Chapters 5 and 6 I examine these expectations with market case studies and novel survey data.

1.5 THE CONTEXT: LAGOS

I test the argument in Lagos, the commercial capital of Nigeria. Markets there typically have a few hundred shops that sell products ranging from cell phones to baby clothes to kitchenware. Some markets focus on one product, while others sell a variety of goods. Most markets are located on land that is either privately held or owned by the local government. Most market leaders are elected and have term limits; others are headed by elected leaders who hold their position for life. Market leaders collect fees from traders that pay for trash collection and security and serve as the liaison between traders and government officials.

Market leaders are critical for promoting trade as courts in Lagos cannot be relied on to enforce contracts or to uphold laws that protect property rights. Over the past fifteen years Lagos state has implemented governance reforms that have increased property rights protection, but these reforms are incomplete and unevenly enforced. Despite some public institutional improvements, the rule of law is weak in Lagos.

With approximately 25 million people,[7] Lagos is a megacity (defined as a city with more than 10 million people). Observers expect it to add 730,000 residents annually in the coming years. Understanding trade in megacities, which are home to roughly 1 in 8 people globally, is important, particularly because most are located in the Global South (*World urbanization prospects the 2014 revision*, 2015, p. 91, 78, 18).

Lagos, which I selected as a research site largely due to the large number of markets with distinct leaders, is an ideal context in which to test existing explanations for private pro-trade policies against my own. Nigeria has a reputation for corrupt governance as well as a vibrant economy; Lagos' GDP is the size of Angola's (Leke et al., 2014, p. 31). A large community of scholars would argue that trade thrives in this context because it takes place *outside* the purview of the government: that it thrives *in spite* of predatory politicians.

I am proposing the opposite: that state threats indirectly generate private trade promotion policies. With hundreds of markets and a number of ways to operationalize state threats, but macro conditions held constant, Lagos allows me to test these two very different predictions head-to-head.

Lagos markets offer two more methodological advantages. First, I am able to see a sometimes elusive counterfactual – markets that fail – because many are on land that the government designates for markets, and alternative use of the land is not normally possible. So unprofitable markets may operate longer than they might in other contexts. Second, some markets have leaders who govern for life, while others have leaders with term limits. This allows me to assess the role of a long time horizon.

1.6 METHODOLOGICAL APPROACH

I use market case studies and survey data to test implications of my argument. The cases will further illuminate the mechanisms driving the relationships between market leader strength, state threats, contractual-trade-promoting policies, and private extortion. The cases will also give evidence of the idiosyncratic determinants of market leader strength and state threats in an attempt to assuage endogeneity concerns and further ensure that there are no omitted

---

[7] Lagos Bureau of Statistics' population estimate as of May 8, 2017.

variables driving the relationships observed in the survey data. Moreover, many studies about informal trade lack a qualitative understanding of micro-level dynamics in marketplaces. The case studies fill this gap.

I draw on original survey data of traders to assess the relationship between state threats and within-market competition, and private good governance. These data improve on prior surveys of small businesses, asking questions about market association membership and how their market leaders govern, which are rarely (if ever) asked. I also improve substantially on prior sampling strategies. Most small business surveys generate a sample frame by collecting a list of firms from a national or municipal statistics agency, but, of course, these lists exclude informal firms that, by definition, do not register with the government. Another approach is to create sampling areas from city blocks (e.g., World Bank, 2010) – for example, by starting at the corner of a given block and approaching the third shop – but poor urban areas may not have clearly defined blocks.

I create a market sample frame that includes the universe of markets in the key commercial areas in Lagos. The starting point for the sample frame was a list of markets from the state trash-collection agency. Their list was missing markets in a few key commercial areas, so research assistants were hired to improve the accuracy of the market listing by mapping the markets in these parts of the city. Research assistants then conducted a census of shops in all of the city's main commercial areas. This resulted in a list of 52,830 shops. After removing shops that were vacant, closed during business hours, or provided services (such as hair salons), a simple random sampling strategy was used to sample from the remaining 24,159 shops and direct traders to specific pre-chosen shops. This shop count resulted in a more complete sample frame than that used for almost any other survey of informal firms. I was able to direct enumerators to specific randomly sampled shops, which greatly reduced the opportunities for enumerator discretion that have plagued prior surveys of informal traders.

The result is a survey that is more representative than earlier surveys of informal traders and includes 199 market associations. Critically, the sample frame is not censored to badly run markets; the markets vary substantially on the outcome – some are very well governed, and some are not.

How do I identify pro-trade policies? Another contribution of this book is to operationalize these policies for measurement in the survey. The survey asks questions about (1) whether leaders represent trader interests, (2) whether market leaders account properly for fees, (3) whether traders feel free to complain to market executives, and (4) whether market leaders had helped traders resolve any disputes in the past year.[8]

In the survey analysis, the primary operationalization for whether markets face state threats comes from whether markets are on local government land, where local politicians have more rights to intervene – more rights to

---

[8] The case studies consider a broader array of trade-promoting policies.

undertake renovations, and a wider set of fees they can collect. However, I will also consider a wider set of threats, including those from police and regulatory agencies.

1.7 OVERVIEW OF THE BOOK

Market associations matter enormously for traders, but these organizations can be opaque to outsiders. This has led to inaccurate perceptions of disorganized informal markets. Chapter 2 justifies the focus on these associations, showing that not only is informal trade organized the world over, but that the modular form is often remarkably similar – with informal trade associations frequently characterized by having an elected leadership committee that includes a head, a treasurer, a secretary, and perhaps a press secretary as well. I then discuss the politics of market associations in Lagos historically and in the twenty-first century, and discuss how market associations can threaten public officials, and vice versa.

Collecting high-quality data that are representative of informal traders presents many difficulties. There were no existing sample frames for the population of interest. Moreover, traders are loath to discuss politics. In Chapter 3 I describe the tools developed for the survey that enabled a careful sampling strategy, data monitoring, and strategies to remove opportunities for enumerator discretion. The strategies discussed in this chapter should inform future data collection among urban populations in the informal sector.

Chapter 4 lays out two critiques of the literature on private governance. First, I show that accounts of private order often ignore the role of leaders by assuming that cooperation is organic. While this might be workable for small groups, leaders are critical in large groups. Second, research on private governance that recognizes the role of leaders stops at proximate explanations for private order. This work largely overlooks the obstacles groups leaders must overcome to, for example, effectively share information about fraudsters. I then expand on the logic of my theory and consider alternative explanations.

In Chapter 5 I test my theory using four market association case studies. One market is a paragon of private good governance, and I assess the conditions that sustain its sophisticated trade-promoting policies. The other three markets have leaders who do not implement trade-promoting policies and are not supportive marketplaces in which to be a trader. One market is an example of a rarely documented but empirically common case in which a market leader extorts from his own traders. Another market is governed by a weak leader who has been unable to push back against government threats. And the final market has a weak leadership characterized by infighting and does not face state threats. Prior research assumes the latter three markets should lose relevance as traders abandon them. For each of these markets, I document the frictions that impede trader relocation.

Chapter 6 tests my argument about competition increasing the hurdles to good private governance by analyzing original data from surveys of 1,179 market traders across 199 market associations in Lagos. The survey data provide details on government threats that markets face, the diversity of products sold in a market – a proxy for competition – and traders' perceptions of how the leaders govern. As important as tests to the main argument, I consider alternative explanations that have never been tested in the context of private governance with a sample of this size.

In Chapter 7 I consider the conditions under which the argument will extend to other types of private groups, such as street vendors in Mexico, the Tehran Bazaar, Ugandan transport associations, slums in Ghana and India, and favelas in Brazil. Some of these groups are characterized by structural factors that more easily constrain leader predation, such as residential associations in which leaders are more embedded in the lives of group members, or groups where switching between organizations is easier, along with regime types that might complicate the theory by making collusion more likely. I also look at whether non-state threats alter group leader incentives in the same way as state threats. I then compare the policy implications of my argument with those of a view in which private pro-trade policies emerge when traders need them. Lastly, I explore the relationship between private good governance in groups and business outcomes for traders and more generalized economic growth in developing countries.

1.8 SUMMARY OF FINDINGS

Both the case and the survey data suggest that government threats make private pro-trade policies more likely. The cases show, first, that private good governance will not always emerge when it is needed. Trade-promoting policies are costly to leaders. Even a benevolent market leader might have competing priorities, and, of course, predatory market leaders exist. In contrast to insinuations from a vast literature on private governance, private trade-promoting policies are not ubiquitous. The cases further suggest that market leader strength is necessary but not sufficient for private good governance. Lastly, the cases show evidence consistent with the second mechanism: the leader of the well-governed market association explicitly states that he punishes his own traders primarily to reduce the likelihood that disputes escalate to the attention of a regulatory agency.

The survey data show that markets on local government land (vs. private land), where politicians have more rights to intervene, are more likely to be better governed. This is surprising given the findings in previous studies that, where politicians' motives are not perceived to be benevolent, private good governance should thrive when these politicians stay out of group affairs. My findings suggest the opposite: that these threats to intervene motivate private good governance. Using a model that controls for whether the market leader holds their position for life, whether the trader has any post-secondary education, the number of employees the trader has, and the value of stock in a trader's shop, the predicted representativeness score is 0.60 for markets on private land and 0.73 for those on local government land. There is also evidence that this effect is stronger when traders are selling different products, and thus are in less direct competition with each other, which makes it easier for leaders to elicit information about customers and suppliers. For markets on local government land, moving from one standard deviation below to one standard deviation above the mean in product diversification increases the predicted representativeness score by 61 percent. There is also support for one of the proposed mechanisms – that leaders will refrain from extorting so as to be able to mobilize traders to credibly threaten public officials. Market political engagement is positively associated with better market leader governance. Finally, the survey data also show that the average trader has been in their shop for over seven years; this number does not vary by market governance. This finding supports my propositions about the barriers to sorting.

A primary contribution of this project is to call into question implicitly functionalist accounts of how contractual trade is enabled when the rule of law is weak. A large body of work has shown that good private governance can promote trade. But prior work can fall into the trap of suggesting that just because these policies enable contractual trade, they will necessarily be implemented. Instead, we need to understand when the obstacles to trade-enabling policies will be overcome, and when they will not. This book focuses on the politics that sustain private pro-trade policies.

2

Market Associations: An Overview

Observers of informal urban markets often describe them as chaotic. Descriptions such as "the chaotic beauty of West African markets"[1] and "chaotic energy"[2] abound. Tourists use similar language; 281 Tripadvisor reviews for a Moroccan market used the word "chaotic." Reviewers wrote: "Words cannot describe the monumental chaos," "My god it's chaos," and "Pure chaos!" This notion of disorganized markets has seeped into the consciousness of many researchers. In economics research on the determinants of firm growth, scholars are often either unaware of how markets are organized or assume associations are irrelevant, focusing instead on individual- and business-level factors.

But what looks or feels chaotic to an outsider is often the opposite. Whether private associations are predatory or supportive of trade, they may regulate every inch of a dense urban market. Traders who sell their goods on a path in front of a shop seeking better access to customers may look like market disorganization, but, in fact, an association governs how far outside the shop they can sell and the fees they pay to do so. Likewise, while hawkers crowding small market paths may not seem to be regulated, an association informally licenses them. Associations play a similarly behind-the-scenes but critical role in spaces like poor neighborhoods and motor parks.

In Chapter 1 I introduced my explanation of variation in private group leadership and described why private leader behavior matters so much for traders in the informal sector. When courts cannot be relied upon to enforce agreements – perhaps in part because the agreements are informal – private associations can help traders avoid fraudsters and deter dishonest behavior. Or they may not, leaving traders vulnerable to a range of scams. Private leaders can help market traders overcome collective action problems by collecting

---

[1] www.dazeddigital.com/art-photography/article/38206/1/lorenzo-vitturi-these-photos-show-the-chaotic-beauty-of-west-african-markets

[2] www.hindustantimes.com/books/this-photographer-captures-the-chaos-of-one-of-the-biggest-street-markets-in-the-world/story-iTithtu9uzLf9xalHTZpyK.html

fees to invest in market security. Or they may extort from association members and pocket the fees instead.

In this chapter I describe the structure of private trade associations around the world. I discuss how such associations are organized in Lagos today, as well as their historical role. In the context of Lagos markets, I show how governments can meddle in the affairs of private associations and how associations can counter these efforts.

I find that the internal organization of trade associations is remarkably similar around the world; even specific executive positions like public relations officers can be found across continents. I demonstrate that, within Lagos, there is only minor variation in the formal titles of association executives; the general structure of these groups is uniform. Next, I show that informal trade associations can be politically important actors everywhere: they can broker votes and liaise with local politicians.

The next part of the chapter highlights the political strength of Lagos markets since the early 1900s. During and after the colonial period, market associations bargained for state services and favorable policies by threatening to mobilize, and ultimately helped the son of their leader gain elected office; he is now one of Nigeria's most influential political patrons. I then show how Lagos state's current modernization agenda trickles down to local governments, creating incentives for politicians to encroach on market affairs, for example, by increasing taxes and closing markets for renovation in order to expand their tax base. Lastly, I show that market associations can sanction government officials with protests and promises to vote for or against particular candidates. Chapter 1 outlined the theoretical importance of government intrusion in private groups. This chapter demonstrates, concretely, how these threats affect associations. Later chapters will show how these dynamics shape private governance.

2.1 MARKETS AND MARKET ASSOCIATIONS IN DEVELOPING COUNTRIES

Market associations, the unit of analysis for this study, are ubiquitous in developing countries. For traders in the informal sector (i.e., those who run businesses that are not registered with all relevant government entities, or do not formally document all transactions) *not* belonging to a market association would be unusual. In La Paz, Bolivia, 75 percent of street vendors – individuals who trade on public land outside of permanent buildings – belong to such associations (Hummel, 2017a, p. 17). In Mexico City, the "vast majority" of street vendors are members of associations (Cross, 1998, p. 120). In my survey of Lagos traders based in plazas (small multistory buildings), 91 percent of traders reported belonging to an association. Research on Lagos street vendors finds an identical percentage – 91 percent – of vendors have an association card (Lawanson, 2014). There is no reason to think these cities are exceptional.

Associations of informal sector traders are so prevalent for two related reasons: members have an external and an internal motivation to join. First, they are vulnerable to government harassment since they must be visible in order to attract customers (Cross, 1998). Organizations allow traders to negotiate with the government without having to incur the costs of formal business registration and tax payment. Associations can help traders negotiate with politicians for space and permission to trade (Cross, 1998). Indeed, governments may even incentivize informal traders to organize to facilitate such negotiations (Hummel, 2017a). Second, organizations can help ensure that suppliers get repaid, customers do not get cheated, disputes get handled, and traders respect each other's right to space (Cross, 1998). However, the existence of an association does not guarantee the presence of these services.

Market associations are important political and economic actors. Market leaders function as liaisons between traders and local politicians. In many cases, politicians have delegated control over access to space in a commercial area to market leaders, who then decide who can and cannot trade there. For example, they have the authority to lock up the shops of traders who do not abide by market rules. Market leaders may also negotiate with politicians over legal and illegal taxes and fees. They may serve as vote brokers, mobilizing traders (who can comprise a substantial portion of the population) to vote for or against certain politicians. Although one of the contributions of my book is to highlight that not all market leaders are strong and that many strong market leaders do not represent the interests of their traders, many such leaders are powerful societal actors. For instance, an official working for the administrative unit that governs Mexico City once described the leader of the largest street vendor association in the city as "very strong. She can stage a rally of 5,000 people in [Mexico City's main square]. If a lower official refused to cooperate with her, she could threaten to pull down a mountain of higher officials on his head" (Cross, 1998, p. 130).

The structure of informal business associations is remarkably similar in different countries. In La Paz, Bolivia, informal street vendor associations have an elected leadership committee, including a secretary general, a treasurer, a secretary, and a "secretary of relations" who often serves as the second-in-command (Hummel, 2017b, pp. 64–65). They may also have a leader who collects donations to help out sick members, or a group of older executives who provide oversight of the executives' management. There are even press secretaries. In Kampala, Uganda, motorcycle taxi drivers are organized into 200–300 local associations, each of which has a chairman, secretary, and treasurer (Goodfellow, 2015).

Across different types and sizes of markets, the structure of market associations within Lagos is remarkably similar. As in many markets around the world, most markets in Lagos have a committee of executives elected by traders based in the market. The head of this committee is sometimes called an *iyaloja* or *babaloja* (market mother or father) or the president or chairman. There may also be a vice-chairman (or deputy to the market mother/father), a secretary, a task force chairman who collects fees from traders, a public relations officer, and a treasurer. There may be an executive who collects donations from traders to pay for a funeral if a fellow trader dies. Some markets have "trustees," market elders who can adjudicate market leadership disputes. Despite some variation across markets in the official titles of these positions, their roles are almost identical.

Despite the critical role market associations play in affecting the businesses of traders, these associations are poorly understood and are rarely incorporated into studies of informality. Economics research on these traders focuses on explaining variation in small-firm growth and why traders may decide to formalize. These studies typically involve analyses that incorporate a series of individual-level covariates (e.g., McPherson, 1996). Some consider variation in the *public* institutional environment (e.g., Mead and Liedholm, 1998; Williams and Shahid, 2016), but they rarely consider the role of private associations for three main reasons. First, associations are often not immediately visible. Many lack formal offices. Or if there is an office, it might lack a sign. Second, there are empirical hurdles to identifying associational membership and determining who belongs to a particular association.[3] The World Bank Enterprise Surveys, which occasionally survey informal traders, do not ask a single question about associational membership, and many scholars of informal firms rely on these data. Third, people tend to think of markets as chaotic; outsiders have a sense that it is each trader for him- or herself. And to some extent this is true. But individualism and competition can (and do) coexist within meaningful associations.

Why do governments allow informality to persist? First, it is important to note that informality is a spectrum. On one end is a trader who is helping to import an illegal drug. On the other end of the spectrum is a trader who sells lightbulbs from a small shop in a market. The latter trader pays local government taxes and is perhaps even located in a market that is on government land. But he or she does not have a business license.

While the more extreme types of illegality are not the focus of this book, there are three general explanations for why governments may intentionally and provisionally fail to enforce regulations against traders. First, the more informal a business, the more vulnerable it is to government extortion. Government officials may personally pocket these illicit fees and thus have an incentive to allow these businesses to remain. Second, informal traders may provide political loyalty in exchange for the intentional nonenforcement of law, which is itself a form of redistribution (Holland, 2016). Alisha Holland estimates that the government is essentially giving a transfer of $1,560 per year to each street vendor in Lima, Peru, by allowing them to continue trading, as that is the amount they save on renting a shop (2015, p. 358). For traders with shops in Lagos, the amount of the transfer would be less – just the value of not having to register one's business – but still nontrivial. Third, by refusing to enforce against informal traders, politicians may be signaling for commitment from poor people for broader constituencies.

---

[3] I will discuss how I dealt with this in Chapter 3.

2.2 HISTORY OF POLITICS AND MARKETS IN LAGOS

Traders have been organized in Lagos since the early 1900s, which makes it an especially appropriate context in which to study variation in private governance. The historical continuity allows me to hold constant trader organization in order to analyze variation in the nature of the organization. The analysis can delve deeper than why and when traders organize, to focus on explaining the characteristics of their associations.

This section traces the political power of trader organizations and the (frequently adversarial) relationships with politicians since the 1920s, when Alimotu Pelewura, a fish trader, became the head of Ereko market, a prominent meat market on Lagos Island. Pelewura led the market with actions that resemble nascent forms of the strategies associations use so effectively today: she could shut down the market to signal the market women's strength, and she collected three pence per week from traders to pay lawyers and clerks who served as intermediaries, translators, and letter writers for interactions with colonial officials (Johnson, 1982).

Pelewura and the market women had a strong relationship with Herbert Macaulay, an early nationalist leader who founded Nigeria's first political party, the Nigerian National Democratic Party (NNDP), in 1923. Macaulay spoke with the market women in Yoruba and showed respect for their traditional leaders and religious associations. He recognized Pelewura's popularity and helped her to create the Lagos Market Women's Guild (Johnson, 1978), which served as the financial backbone of the NNDP from the 1920s to the 1940s (Sklar, 2004).

While Macaulay collaborated with the Guild, the colonial administration saw the market women's organization, and in particular the efficiently run Ereko market, as a threat. Some colonial officials argued that the market association should provide more of a social function, and not collect fees or perform internal sanctioning functions (Johnson, 1978). But even social functions were not without controversy. When Pelewura was planning to close the markets so that the traders could perform a play, colonial officials argued (unsuccessfully) that she did not have the right to do so. The colonial administration correctly perceived Pelewura's strength as a threat.

In the 1930s, Pelewura, serving as the representative of sixteen markets, was appointed to the local *Ilu* committee, which comprised representatives of societal groups that reported to the *oba*, or traditional king. While Nigerian politicians continued to work *with* the powerful market women, the colonial administration repeatedly proposed policies that alienated them. Pelewura successfully fought off colonial attempts to relocate Ereko market – a threat markets face to this day, as "modernizing" state officials work to put traders into physically delimited areas zoned for trading and to reallocate property in space-constrained Lagos.

In 1932 rumors circulated that the colonial administration planned to start taxing the Lagos market women. The market women met to discuss this and sent representatives to colonial officials, who quickly assured them there was no truth to these rumors. In the late 1930s, however, in an effort to raise funds for World War II, the administration did indeed try to start taxing women who made more than fifty pounds per year. In 1940, under the leadership of Pelewura and Rabiatu Alaso Oke, the *iyalode* (among the highest traditional Yoruba titles given to women), market women protested at the colonial commissioner office. They argued that (1) it went against local custom to tax women, (2) unlike British women, who paid taxes, African women were poor, and (3) the women had no vote in Lagos and thus should not be asked to pay taxes. Traditional rulers in Lagos strongly supported the women's protest. When the commissioner ignored their demands, the market women closed the markets, which was a remarkable signal of their strength. The protest largely succeeded. Bernard Henry Bourdillon, the governor at the time who was on close terms with the early nationalist leaders, agreed to tax only women who made more than 200 pounds per year, which was a very small portion of traders (Johnson, 1982).

The market women exercised their strength again in fighting price controls. In 1939, at the start of World War II, a variety of factors, including a decline in farm laborers caused by men moving to the cities, contributed to a food shortage. In 1941 the colonial administration introduced the Pullen marketing scheme, an attempt to implement price controls for food products. Throughout the early 1940s Pelewura led the fight against the price controls, utilizing new strategies along with old strategies that had served her well in dealing with previous challenges. The initial response was to simply defy the scheme, and the colonial administration was largely unable to enforce its policies. In October 1943 the colonial administration took a new approach: buying up large quantities of food and selling it at a set price, essentially subsidizing transport and other costs. In response, the Lagos market women physically disrupted the trucks transporting this food and convinced producers to sell to the traders as opposed to government officials (Oyemakinde, 1973). Pelewura mobilized the support of Macaulay, his NNDP, and the traditional rulers of Lagos and threatened to shut down the markets. Colonial officials tried to buy off Pelewura, offering her a monthly salary of more than seven pounds if she would assist in the price scheme implementation; she refused (Johnson, 1982).

In 1958, two years before independence, the nascent Action Group party began attempting to incorporate markets into its party structure. Party officials set up party structures inside markets (Sklar, 2004, p. 436). At this time, decisions were being made to transform two areas of Lagos Island into markets. While traders were working to understand the stall allocation process, the Lagos Town Council realized it had underestimated the cost of making these low-lying areas suitable for trade. The Action Group began working in concert with the cash-strapped Town Council to make stall allocation conditional on Action Group membership (Rapson, 1959). The confusion surrounding the allocation process and fees provided the first opportunity for the market women to demonstrate that they could organize themselves after Pelewura's death in 1951.

In November 1958 the market women petitioned the governor to express their concern about (among other things) the politically driven allocation of market stalls. They succeeded in spurring a colonial report on the topic, which ordered the return to an apolitical stall allocation process (Rapson, 1959).

Abibat Mogaji became leader of the Lagos Market Women Association (LMWA) in the 1980s. This organization has since morphed into the Market Men and Women Association, an umbrella group for the smaller market associations that are the focus of this project. Mogaji's son, Ashiwaju Ahmed Bola Tinubu, became the governor of Lagos following Nigeria's return to democracy in 1999. Bola Tinubu represented the Alliance for Democracy party, the latest incarnation of the Action Group party, and the precursor to the modern All Progressives Congress (APC) party. Many have attributed his gubernatorial victory to his mother's ability to mobilize traders in support of his candidacy.

Following Mogaji's death in 2013, her granddaughter, Bola Tinubu's daughter, Folashade Tinubu-Ojo, became the new *iyaloja* general for Lagos.[4] The Peoples Democratic Party (PDP) (which at the time controlled the federal government, but was in the opposition in Lagos) protested Tinubu-Ojo's appointment, citing it as evidence of what it claimed were the dictatorial tendencies of Babatunde Fashola, Lagos' APC governor at the time.[5] Their concerns about political influence over this umbrella organization were well founded, but nothing came of their protests.

In short, market organization in Lagos has been characterized by remarkable continuity in politician interest in markets. Politicians' threats against markets – whether related to relocation or taxation – have been a challenge for decades. Similarly, market threats against government officials have persisted since the colonial period.

2.3 CONTEMPORARY LAGOS MARKET ASSOCIATIONS

Nigeria has a federal system of government, with 36 states and over 800 local governments. Lagos state, which encompasses the city of Lagos, is the country's commercial center. It has about 25 million residents, tens of thousands of traders, and 57 local governments (see Figure 2.1). Local governments have jurisdiction over the markets, which are located on both public and private land. The Nigerian constitution mandates that local governments maintain and regulate markets and permits local governments to collect taxes from market traders.

Market associations operate in the shadow of complicated Lagos state government objectives. Local political leaders have dramatically increased the effectiveness of tax collection to further their aim to transform it into a modernized city that is not dependent on the federal government for revenue. These goals influence local politicians' incentives when interacting with

---

4 "General" connotes being the mother of multiple markets.
5 Interview with Lagos state PDP officials on July 1, 2013.

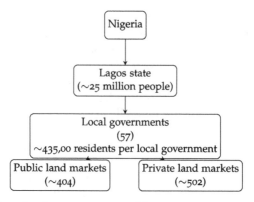

FIGURE 2.1 Markets, local governments, and Lagos state

markets. Local politicians aim to modernize markets and increase tax revenue from them, while retaining the support of market associations.

How much do traders pay in taxes? The average trader in my data reports paying $40 per year in local government fees, and the modal trader reports paying $18 annually. Aggressive efforts in recent years by the Lagos state government to get informal traders on the state tax roll have resulted in some informal traders paying state taxes as well. These are flat rates (for informal traders), and at the time of research capped at $30 annually. On the one hand, these numbers may seem high; the traders are, after all, typically not registered with the government, so maybe it is surprising they are paying any taxes at all. On the other hand, given that the modal trader reports paying almost $14,000 per year for the goods that they sell, these numbers seem low. The local tax rates are likely the maximum amount that local governments can collect without so angering markets that it results in political backlash. The state government, for its part, at the time of research, prioritized simply getting traders on the tax roll and was less concerned with the actual amount paid.

The modal Lagos market association in my study has 200 traders. Figure 2.6 shows a commercial area that consists of many market associations. These markets sell products ranging from mobile phones to baby clothes to kitchenware. In many respects, market association governance is quite formal. Most associations – even weak ones – have written constitutions, and every trader has their own copy. See Figure 2.4 for a photo of the cover of a market association constitution. Sometimes the constitutions are just two pages long, a printed-out Microsoft Word document describing market association fees, the punishment for nonpayment, and the fines associated with fighting in the market.[6]

Some constitutions are longer; the constitution pictured in Figures 2.2 and 2.3 is seventy-two pages long. This constitution sets out the rules governing the relationship between traders. It describes how theft is dealt with and outlines

---

[6] Appendix A shows the structure of informal trade in Lagos.

**SECTION 13 - REVENUE /
LEVY COLLECTORS COMMITTEE**

a. The executive committee shall institute a levy collectors committee. They all must be financial up to-date members.

b. Appointed members of this committee shall be presented to the general house at the general meeting for ratification.

c. It shall constitute of not less than five (5) and not more than seven (7) members and must have stock in the market.

d. They shall on assumption of duty sign an undertaking to indemnify the association of any embezzlement or misappropriation for which he is found guilty. The association reserves the right to recover such sums from his stocks in the market or personal effect.

e. Must return all revenue collected to the financial secretary within forty-eight (48) hours of collection.

**SECTION 14 - DUTIES OF REVENUE / LEVY
COLLECTORS COMMITTEE**

i. Collection of all levies such as Nepa and Security Levys, berial levy and others as contained in the constitution or as may be decided by the general meeting or the executive committee.

ii. Shall as collet monthly Nepa and Security Levies of N1000= from shops and N500 from attachment and N200 from field users or other sum as may be approved by the Association from time to time.

iii Shall handover all monies collected to the financial secretary within the stipulated time and collect receipt for such payments and keep it for audit purposes.

iv. Shall pay fines as stipulated in article 5 section (e) where money collected are not paid as at when due.

v. Shall not serve for more than two (2) tenures consecutively.

vi. Shall perform other responsibilities that pertain to levy matters as may be directed by the executive committee.

FIGURE 2.2 Excerpt of a Lagos market association constitution: revenue collection

ii. Drawing the attention of a customer who is at another's shop attracts a fine of Two Thousand Naira (N2,000.00)

iii. Unauthorized tampering with a customer's vehicle attracts a fine of Five Thousand Naira (N5,000.00)

iv. Any person(s) found guilty of acting or conniving with a servant/apprentice to steal his master's money/goods or that of another person shall be made to refund all such money or goods and also pay a fine of Fifty Thousand Naira (N50,000.00)

v. In order to discourage fighting in the market, any two people found fighting whether an apprentice or master must be made to pay a fine of Two Thousand Naira (N2,000.00) each before their matter "will be looked into. After which the offender will forfeit his N2,000.00 while his partner will forfeit N1,000.00 as cost of fighting. That is. One Thousand Naira (N1,000.00) should be refunded to him. Anyone found to have fought up to three (3) times (a notorious offender) should be suspended for one week or a longer period.

vi. Anybody who tries to initiate a fight by slapping, hitting, pushing, kicking or holding another person will be made to pay a find of Two Thousand Naira

FIGURE 2.3 Excerpt of a Lagos market association constitution: sanctions

the fines for traders who tug at the clothes of a customer to try to get their attention. The constitution describes the process of market leadership elections, the roles of different market executives, who is eligible to contest, as well as the process for changing the constitution.

The most meaningful variation between market constitutions in Lagos is the term of the elected leaders: leaders of older associations tend to have terms for life, while heads of newer groups have terms of a few years and are subjected to term limits.

FIGURE 2.4 Oke Arin Market constitution
Notes: This photo is used with the permission of the market president. The constitution excerpts shown in Figures 2.2 and 2.3 are from a different market.

For some "traditional" markets in Lagos – that is, those in a physically delimited plot of land where traders sell fruits and vegetables on wooden stands in addition to shops – the bounds of the market and market association are obvious. The plot of land demarcates the market, and there will be one main association for the area. This association will typically have the same name as the market. For example, if the market is called Pelewura, the association will be called the Pelewura market association, or traders might reference the Pelewura market executives.

But it is not always this straightforward. For traders in plazas – multistory buildings with 10–50 traders in small shops – one cannot assume that the association for that building is the traders' main market association. For example, Figure 2.5 shows Trade Fair, a large commercial area in Lagos. Each gray rectangle is a plaza. While there are typically associations for each plaza, there

FIGURE 2.5 Satellite image of Trade Fair. Source: Google Earth

Notes: Trade Fair is a commercial area in Lagos. Each gray rectangle is a plaza, but the plaza association is not always a trader's main business association.

are also often associations for clusters of plazas. In addition, there are three main associations in Trade Fair: the Balogun Business Association, the Association of Progressive Traders, and the Auto Spare Parts and Machinery Dealers Association, as well as an association for all of Trade Fair.

There are additional complications. Sometimes a market association is best conceptualized as the landlord of the land on which traders are trading. Other times, a largely absentee landlord coexists with a democratically elected association, which is the more relevant association for traders. In Chapter 3 I describe how I address associational membership empirically.

There are additional associations within market areas, but none that are as consistently important as the general market association. Commodity unions, for example, are associations for traders within a market selling the same product. Commodity unions typically exist for price fixing, but traders report they are rarely effective at enforcing prices. There may also be ethnic associations, or associations based on which state in Nigeria traders trace their ancestry to.

2.3.1 Impact of Lagos's Model City Ambitions on Local Politicians' Incentives

Local government power in Nigeria is concentrated in the chairman, who is directly elected by local citizens and who appoints the heads of department within the local government (Barkan, Gboyega and Stevens, 2001). The APC party dominates all branches and levels of government in Lagos state. In Nigeria, where the party that controls the state government typically controls all local governments in the state, the most critical hurdle for aspiring

FIGURE 2.6 Balogun commercial area, Lagos Island
Notes: Balogun consists of many distinct market associations. This photo was taken by Sunday
Alamba and is used here with his permission.

local government chairmen is getting the party's nomination rather than the
elections.

If local chairmen aspire to higher public office – for example, more presti-
gious positions in the state government – they need to impress the APC leaders.
These leaders reward chairmen for (1) increasing internally generated revenue,
(2) doing so without antagonizing powerful societal groups, such as powerful
market associations, and (3) modernizing their communities.

Political leaders in Lagos promote economic growth, infrastructure development, social development and security, and environmental sustainability[7]
in an effort to make the state an African Model City, a local term for a city
"that is a global, economic and financial hub, safe, secured, functional and
productive."[8] Political competition between the state and federal government
motivated Lagos's political leaders to aim for autonomy and Model City status. Lagos's Model City goals require a delicate balance of activities. Political
leaders seek to strike a delicate balance between raising taxes and maintaining
(and strengthening) popular support. For instance, the state wants to remove
informal settlements without alienating powerful voting blocs, and to improve
traffic without upsetting the powerful transport union (de Gramont, 2014).

[7] Lagos State Government, Aligning Medium Term Sector Strategy with Lagos State Development Plan, November 2014, available at www.sparc-nigeria.com/RC/files/1.2.14_Aligning
_MTSS_with_LSDP_Report_November_2014.pdf, accessed January 31, 2018.
[8] Lagos State Development Plan, 2012–2015.

To promote development, the state government aims to "create [a] conducive investment environment with a view to making Lagos state the preferred investment destination in Sub-Saharan Africa" in part by "improving perceptions of Lagos as an attractive and prosperous African city."[9] These efforts involve "mega projects" – complex long-term projects initiated by the government and implemented by private contractors, often in coordination with many domestic and international stakeholders.[10] For instance, informal settlements have been demolished to make way for Lagos Rail Mass Transit – a system that includes a 28 km monorail. In May 2016 a $1 billion partnership was announced with a Japanese agency to build a monorail to connect other parts of the city.[11] Billions of dollars are being invested in Eko Atlantic, a massive development project built on land reclaimed from the ocean that will be essentially a luxury extension of Lagos – it has been compared to Fifth Avenue in New York.[12]

While civil society groups have highlighted the many ways in which the city's megacity ambitions threaten the livelihoods of poor people,[13] political elites are unified around these goals. The state has a long time horizon and is willing and able to invest resources into building mega projects.[14]

Lagos state has historically been governed by the APC and its precursors. From the start of the Third Republic (1999–2015), the federal government was continuously controlled by the PDP. The APC had a relatively strong hold over Lagos (and some other southwestern states) but was not competitive at the federal level.

Bola Tinubu (currently the informal head of the APC and a powerful figure known locally as "the godfather") was elected governor of Lagos state in 1998. He quickly garnered a reputation for "shaking things up." For example, he alienated party elders by appointing technocrats to head state

9 SPARC, Lagos: Yesterday, Today and Tomorrow, February 2014, available at sparc-nigeria.com/RC/files/5.4.11-Introducing-the-Lagos-State-Development-Plan.html, accessed January 31, 2018.

10 Heinrich Boll Stiftung Nigeria and Fabulous Urban, Urban Planning Processes in Lagos, 2016, available at ng.boell.org/sites/default/files/uploads/2016/02/160206_urban_planning_processes_digital_new.pdf, accessed January 31, 2018.

11 *This Day*, "Lagos to Partner Japan on Construction of $1bn Marina-Ikoyi-Lekki Monorail Project," May 10, 2016, available at thisdaylive.com/index.php/2016/05/10/lagos-to-partner-japan-on-construction-of-1bn-marina-ikoyi-lekki-monorail-project/, accessed January 31, 2018.

12 This is according to a manager of a construction unit under the group heading the development. Drew Hinshaw, "Nigerian Developer Set to Build Africa's Next Giant City," *Wall Street Journal*, August 12, 2013, available at www.wsj.com/articles/SB10001424127887324251504578581570831563906, accessed January 31, 2018.

13 Heinrich Boll Stiftung Nigeria and Fabulous Urban 2016; Adam Nossiter, "In Nigeria's Largest City, Homeless Are Paying the Price of Progress," March 1, 2013, available at www.nytimes.com/2013/03/02/world/africa/homeless-pay-the-price-of-progress-in-lagos-nigeria.html?_r=0, accessed January 31, 2018.

14 The state government very much embodies Evans' (1995) notion of embedded autonomy.

ministries (de Gramont, 2014). His relationship with the then president Olusegun Obasanjo quickly became contentious as Tinubu vied for increased autonomy for Lagos state. Efforts to increase the number of local governments in Lagos became the most salient dispute with the federal government, and ultimately Tinubu created thirty-seven new local governments without federal permission; as of mid-2018 these local governments were still not formally recognized by the federal government.

Lagos' self-sufficiency is not due solely to the fact that it is the largest commercial area in the country. Maintaining independence from the federal government has also required increasing internally generated revenue to decrease dependence on monthly oil revenue allocations.[15] Between 2005 and 2014, Lagos increased its internally generated revenue from N35 billion (about $97 million) to N245 billion (just over $681 million) (Awam, 2014, p. 297). Since 2007 federal allocations have constituted less than half of Lagos' budgetary needs, which is far less than other Nigerian states (Awam, 2014, p.27) (see Figure 2.7).

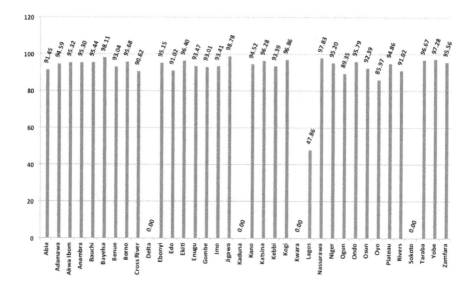

Note: Data not available in respect of Delta, Kaduna, Kwara and Sokoto States
Source of Data: Joint Tax Board

A presentation by The Executive Chairman   56

FIGURE 2.7 State-level financial dependence on federal allocations (%), 2008
Notes: Source: Lagos Internal Revenue Service.

[15] Even though the APC gained control of the federal government in 2015, these goals still hold today as the PDP could regain the presidency in the future.

2.3.2 How Strong Market Leaders Can Sanction State Officials

My argument is that market leaders will govern well when they can threaten public officials, including politicians, and when these officials can in turn make their own threats. Markets can respond to the prospect of tax hikes and modernization threats with protests and vote mobilization. When local politicians have higher ambitions in government, these actions are embarrassing. They want to show the state government that they are capable of getting communities to go along with their reforms. This dynamic deters market leaders from extorting from their traders: they need to keep traders on their side in order to mobilize them against state intrusion. It also incentivizes leaders to reduce disputes in the market to limit opportunities for rent-seeking by public officials.

What do these threats look like? In this section I discuss the power market leaders can hold over local politicians. Market leaders know that ambitious local politicians aim to please Bola Tinubu, the de facto leader of the APC who controls the party's nomination process. One way they can frustrate these politicians is to protest. Tinubu has few reliable ways of getting information about public satisfaction with the local government. If a market leader shuts down the market for a day and persuades traders to protest against local politicians' actions, perhaps at the governor's mansion, it would send a clear and credible signal to state party officials of dissatisfaction with local governance.

According to Tinubu:

[T]raders act as reliable sources of information for the government and political parties ... [and] serve as the crucial feedback mechanism needed by the government and policy makers to evaluate instituted and proposed policies.[16]

Protests hurt chairmen seeking renomination. According to the 2014 Lagos state APC Chairman Henry Ajomale:

Traders can prevent a chairman from getting renominated. We take cognizance of that. If we reappoint such a person we will run into trouble. In Alimosho [one Lagos local government] we picked someone, people protested, so we gave the nomination to someone else. This was before the election. We have done this so many times.[17]

Market leaders can also sanction politicians through voter mobilization. Some market leaders and traders vote in primaries, which gives them a powerful voice.[18] Market leaders can also mobilize traders to "vote as a bloc" in general elections. Traders are also seen as effective mobilizers for their acquaintances: "They spread support of the APC even in their homes," the local politician said.[19]

"Shop sleeping" is another tactic market leaders can use to support a preferred candidate. In Nigeria, no vehicle movement is permitted on election day:

---

[16] Interview by email on February 5, 2014.
[17] Interview on January 20, 2014.
[18] Interview with local politician B on March 13, 2017.
[19] Interview with local politician B on March 13, 2017.

citizens are supposed to register and vote where they live. Many traders do not live in the same jurisdiction as their market. Market leaders who can mobilize traders can arrange for them to sleep in their shops the night before election day, and vote as a bloc in support of a politician.[20]

When asked what constrained a local government from renovating a market – which would price out existing traders – one local government chairman told me he "negotiates with traders because they are voters. And some of them are party members; you don't want public outcry."[21] While market traders cannot always prevent an APC-nominated candidate from getting elected, the APC wants organized societal groups to support its leadership. Protests or losing large groups of voters is embarrassing for the APC.

While the APC in Lagos has been dominant in recent years at the state and local levels, it is still important for local politicians to achieve high vote shares. This allows the party to claim a mandate for the broad reforms its leaders strive to execute. At the local government level, for those running for chairmen or incumbent chairmen running for reelection, a high vote share signals local popularity, a reliable metric for party leaders strategizing about who to support for higher office down the line. Moreover, in recent local government elections the PDP has come close to winning some chairmen positions. Thus, winning votes may matter purely for electoral success as well.

2.3.3   How State Officials Can Sanction Markets

Local politicians, in turn, have their own strategies for threatening markets, which are based on their constitutional authority to tax and "maintain" markets. For example, they can threaten to kick out all of a market's traders in order to "renovate" markets. The market would be demolished, and maybe two or three years later it would be rebuilt as a multistory plaza. The original traders can rarely afford shops in the new market, which might be N500,000 ($1,389)/year, compared to N100,000 ($278)/year in the original market.[22]

Local politicians can also threaten to raise taxes. Market leaders will rarely view efforts to increase taxes on traders as anything but a threat. Local politicians may promise to reinvest tax revenue in the markets or to invest in public services like road repair that would benefit traders. But these promises are rarely credible. Based on their history of interaction with the local government, traders view these politicians as predatory.

Being on local government land makes markets increasingly vulnerable to each of these threats. Local politicians have greater rights to intervene in or renovate these markets. It would be difficult for a local government chairman to threaten to demolish a market on private land. Additionally, while local governments are limited to a certain amount of fees they can collect from

---

[20] Interviews with trader R on January 22, 2015, and with local politician B on March 13, 2017.
[21] Interview with local politician C on January 12, 2013.
[22] Interview with local politician B on March 13, 2017.

traders in both types of markets, they often collect rent from traders in public markets; threats to raise rents are considered serious.

Markets may face threats emanating from government entities besides the local government. For example, certain state or federal agencies can be empowered to intervene in markets depending on the product sold.

2.4 CONCLUSION

This chapter described markets and market associations in developing countries in general, and then in Lagos in particular over the past century. I discussed the politics of modern market associations in Lagos, and how markets can threaten public officials, and vice versa.

Discussions of Lagos's modernizing ambitions raise a question regarding the scope of this book's argument. The scope conditions for this project are contexts in which the rule of law is weak, but not absent. Certainly, the rule of law is not absent in Lagos, and over the past fifteen years, Lagos state has implemented meaningful governance reforms that have increased the protection of property rights. Have these improvements in governance pushed Lagos outside the scope of the project?

They have not. These reforms have been incomplete and unevenly enforced. For example, the average number of days to resolve a standard commercial dispute in a Lagos court has dropped to 447 days – below even the average for Cape Town, South Africa – but the average cost of resolution in Lagos is 62 percent of the claim value, compared to 34 percent in Cape Town (World Bank, 2014). Independent state audits of local government accounts have been introduced to increase local accountability, but these reports still regularly reveal huge sums of unaccounted money (Office of State Auditor General, 2012). In 2011 a law was passed prohibiting street hawkers, a priority for many market traders who lose business to them, but in recent years enforcement has waned and street hawkers are visible throughout the city. In short, despite some public institutional improvements, Lagos still falls within the scope condition of the theory as a city in which the rule of law is weak.

3

Conducting a Representative Survey of Informal Traders

"What is your main market or plaza association?" an enumerator asks a trader. "I don't belong to any association," the trader replies. "Do you attend any market meetings?" the enumerator follows up, but the trader says no. "So who do you pay trash collection fees to?" the enumerator probes. "I pay trash fees to the market executive," the trader answers. "Ah, so you *do* have an association," the enumerator says. "Yes, there are executives, but they do not help me in any way."

A version of the aforementioned conversation occurred dozens of times in the course of the trader survey discussed in this chapter. The dialogue highlights the challenges to identifying associations and associational membership – challenges that exist for many types of groups, not just market associations. Traders may say they are not part of an association, but they do belong to a union, which in this context is a matter of semantics. One trader may say an association does not have a name, while another may belong to the 8 Idowu Lane Plaza Association, and both associations are the same thing. When working to determine who belongs to the same association, these challenges are salient.

It is absolutely critical to determine whether traders who at first say they do not belong to an association in fact do. These traders are more likely to belong to ineffective associations, and these associations are important to identify to facilitate comparisons with the associations that have trade-promoting policies. It is these less active associations, I argue, that have received less attention from researchers.

Chapter 2 highlighted the importance of private trade associations for individuals in the informal sector and showed how local politicians shape group leader incentives. I developed my theory of private governance inductively through many months of interviews with traders, market leaders, and government officials in Lagos. These interviews brought me to markets in Lagos Island, a central, densely populated commercial area with substantial pedestrian traffic where traders pay high rents. But the interviews also brought me to quiet markets on the outskirts of the city that took three hours to reach with traffic. I interviewed traders with thousands of dollars of secondhand laptops in their shops, as well as those who sold fish. I went to local government offices where the generator stayed on all day, providing constant power, and a professional team of civil servants worked for a reformist chairman who was willing to speak openly about issues in the community. But at 11 am, I also visited local government offices that had no power, where respondents were secretive and distrustful. Since I was careful to visit people not only in accessible places but also parts of the city, my theory was informed by a diverse array of perspectives.

I proceeded to test the theory with a survey of traders, which I wanted to be just as representative. This chapter takes up Auerbach et al.'s (2018) call for researchers to develop creative strategies to overcome obstacles to data collection in urban and informal spaces. I discuss the strategies I developed to help inform future data collection efforts in the informal sector. Conducting a representative survey of informal traders that produces high-quality data entails many challenges. For instance, most studies of small businesses rely on lists of firms from government agencies. But how can we create a sample frame when informal traders are, by definition, not registered with the government? The few existing surveys of informal traders rely on sampling protocols that ultimately allow enumerators to approach friendly traders. How, then, to create a sampling strategy that removes opportunities for enumerator discretion? Traders are also very busy and loathe discussing politics. How can we collect meaningful data from this population?

In this chapter, I describe how I collected representative and high-quality data. I describe a trader census I managed of tens of thousands of shops. I then randomly sampled from this census and could direct enumerators to specific shops, reducing the likelihood that – for example – an enumerator avoids a shop where a trader is busy and picks the shop without customers. I describe how I used WhatsApp to communicate with traders who questioned whether enumerators were who they said they were, a common challenge in contexts of high distrust. I show how I used auditors not just to reask a subset of the survey questions but also to assess whether enumerators followed the sampling protocol. And lastly, I describe the brute-force approach to defining market association membership, which involved returning to traders to determine whether, for example, the Balogun Market Association was the same as the Balogun Trade Association.

The protocols discussed in this chapter have broad implications for data collection for other informal populations. While the census was time-consuming, in urban areas, research assistants can reach populations quicker than in rural areas, increasing the number of people or shops that assistants count per day. While sampling is always difficult, sampling informal populations has a special set of issues. In slums, for example, researchers cannot direct enumerators to formal numbered street addresses. The strategies I describe to audit the sampling strategy – something that is rarely done – could be easily tacked on to existing auditing protocols for large gains without adding much cost.

3.1 SURVEYING INFORMAL TRADERS: SAMPLING AND RECRUITMENT

To test the theory, I needed data from traders. I rely on the first round of the Lagos Trader Survey, a survey of plaza traders that I conducted in 2015. In this section, I describe challenges for scholars interested in surveying urban traders, how these challenges have typically been dealt with in past studies, and the novel strategies I used in my 2015 survey.

3.1.1 Creating a Sample Frame of Traders

The Problem

There are two difficulties associated with creating a sample frame of microenterprises: small firms that may or may not be registered, may or may not pay various taxes and likely have no employees or just one employee. The first is determining the universe of markets, particularly in a city that might have hundreds of markets. It is not obvious where to find a list of markets, as they are also unlikely to register with the government.

The second difficulty is creating a sample frame for traders within these markets. Even if a market-level sample frame has been created, it is just as complicated to identify the universe of traders within an association. For one, the physical boundaries of what outsiders think of as "the market" might not completely overlap with the bounds of an association. Moreover, market leaders rarely divulge the number of traders in their association. Lists of traders are among a leader's most valuable and sensitive information: they are motivated to understate the true number of traders to tax collectors and to prevent government officials from enumerating the market.

Examples of Solutions from the Literature

The 2009 World Bank Enterprise Survey in Nigeria included just ten microenterprises in each state and limited the sample frame to "the busiest streets and markets" (2009, p. 7, footnote 5). This approach is problematic, because microenterprises in prominent locations are likely not representative of all microenterprises.

However, there have been impressive attempts to create sample frames in other types of markets. Tariq Thachil created a sample frame of meeting places in Delhi, India, where informal labor workers gather to find employment by starting with a list of these places from a government board responsible for the safety of construction workers (2017, appendix, p. 39).

My Approach

To create my market-level sample frame, I started with a list of markets from the Lagos Waste Management Authority, the state trash collection agency. Because this agency collects trash from markets and because the state government subsidizes the collection, even poorer markets are included on its lists. Their list included 502 plazas (which are a type of marketplace).

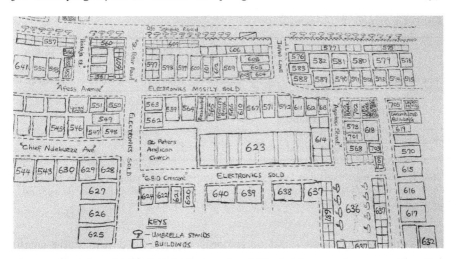

FIGURE 3.1 Map of part of Alaba International Market for sampling

Notes: Aluko Abubakar Olanrewaju, a research assistant, drew this map. He and other research assistants counted the shops in each part of the market. Enumerators were then instructed (for example) to go to building 616 in the market, walk up to the second floor, turn right, and find the third mobile phone shop.

While the plaza list seemed fairly complete, it was missing plazas in a few key commercial areas,[1] and some places that were called plazas were, in essence, large commercial areas with many plazas. I hired a research assistant to map out both the missing areas and the areas that were called plazas but were, in fact, much larger than a typical plaza.[2]

To determine the universe of traders within these plazas, I hired research assistants to count the number and types of shops in every plaza, resulting in a listing of 52,830 shops. This shop count resulted in a more complete sample frame than that used for almost any other survey of informal firms. The structure of the listing data is shown in Table 3.1.

3.1.2 Sampling Traders from the Sample Frame

The Problem, and How Previous Studies Have Addressed It

Sampling traders within a commercial area is difficult without a census of traders. Some World Bank Enterprise Surveys of microenterprises use a city-block sampling strategy in which enumerators are instructed to stand at the corner of a specific city block, face north, and approach the fourth shop on the left.

The problem with this approach is that it imposes a level of order on dense urban environments that may not be realistic. In Lagos, commercial areas do not have a Manhattan grid-style structure to their streets. Roads turn.

---

[1] This may be because these areas had their own lists that I did not obtain.
[2] These included Alaba (pictured in Figure 3.1).

TABLE 3.1 *Structure of census data*

Plaza name	Address	Floor #	# shops selling textiles	# shops selling jewelry	# shops providing services
Goodluck Plaza	132 Adewale St., Lagos Island	0	5	9	0
Goodluck Plaza	132 Adewale St., Lagos Island	1	0	0	5

Notes: The shop count resulted in a data set with information on the number of shops on each floor in each plaza, along with information on the types of products being sold. The data shown here are fake, and many other product categories are included in the real data.

Small paths connect areas, and these paths may be lined with thirty small shops. Some areas might have multistory buildings, and it is not clear how the Enterprise Surveys handle such idiosyncrasies.

More careful approaches to sampling in informal contexts can be observed in studies of residents in urban areas that include informal settlements, and in a survey of street vendors. These surveys have divided an urban area into small spatial clusters. Within each cluster, a random GPS point (or street) is selected as the starting point. From this starting point, enumerators follow a random walk protocol (Hummel, 2017a, appendix, p. 11; Nathan, 2016, appendix, p. 9; Paller, 2015).

While these approaches increase the likelihood of reaching respondents in informal settlements – and informal traders, in the case of Hummel – Thachil's sampling strategy also successfully reduces opportunities for enumerator discretion. Enumerators may be tempted to approach more friendly traders (or residents, or laborers), or less busy traders, or those who have a fan or chair in their shop. Yet these traders could be unrepresentative on any number of dimensions. In Thachil's survey of laborers in their meeting place, respondents were sampled by handing out essentially lottery tickets as people entered the meeting place. He then conducted a drawing that revealed who would be invited to participate in the survey (2017, appendix, p. 39). Similarly, in a survey of informal settlement residents, Adam Auerbach directed enumerators to specific households identified from satellite data (2017).

My Sampling Approach

My trader census made the sampling relatively straightforward. I removed from the census any shops that were vacant, closed during business hours, or provided services (such as a hair salon), and then randomly sampled from the remaining 24,159 shops. For example, I might sample a textile shop on the second floor of a specific plaza.

The next step was more complicated. If the textile shop was one of three textile shops on a particular floor of the plaza, I wanted to direct the enumerator to a *specific* one in order to reduce enumerator discretion. But I could not provide additional information on the shop. After all, I only knew that

FIGURE 3.2 Photo of two traders who participated in the 2015 survey
Notes: They are standing in front of their shops, which are on Lagos Island. The photo was taken by Sunday Alamba, and is used here with his permission.

there were three textile shops on a particular floor. So I randomly sampled a number between 1 and the total number of textile shops on that floor, and then randomly sampled "left" or "right." Enumerators would then be instructed to enter the second floor of the plaza, turn left, and approach the second textile shop, for instance. If the trader was not able to participate when approached, the enumerator would return multiple times in later weeks to attempt to hold the interview.

3.1.3 Convincing Traders to Participate in the Survey

The Problem, and How Previous Studies Have Approached It
Thachil highlights one challenge of worksite-based surveying: respondents may be busy (2018). Indeed, Lagos traders tend to be very busy in their shops. Because the modal shop has no employees, traders typically cannot leave their shop during business hours since there is no one to help them attend to customers. Moreover, there is distrust in these environments. Traders have been surveyed by people claiming to be academics, only to learn later that they were businessmen researching market opportunities.

It is difficult to assess how these obstacles are typically dealt with. The World Bank Enterprise Survey does not explicitly describe how it deals with these challenges for microenterprises. These problems may be mitigated by enumerators approaching friendly traders, but that, of course, is no solution at all.

My Approach to Encouraging Survey Participation

To incentivize traders to take the time to participate in the interview while simultaneously managing their shop, I used four strategies. First, the enumerator provided N400 ($1.11) of prepaid phone credit to the respondent at the end of the survey. Second, at the start of the interview enumerators gave traders a folder branded with the name of the survey (Lagos Trader Survey), along with a pamphlet with information on business etiquette in countries that Lagos traders travel to, like China and the United Arab Emirates. Since many of these traders travel when importing, I suspected this information would be interesting to them. Third, enumerators provided respondents with a sheet of paper with my collaborator's, project manager's, and my WhatsApp numbers and BlackBerry Messenger pins and encouraged traders to reach out to us. By the end of the survey, the three of us had chatted informally with 93 traders who had contacted us using these platforms, often to verify the legitimacy of the enumerators. Fourth, we assured traders that we would provide a report summarizing the survey findings; we delivered the reports when we resurveyed them in 2016. The effective response rate for the survey was 81 percent, providing data from 1,179 traders.

3.2 POLICING THE SAMPLING STRATEGY AND INCOMING DATA

3.2.1 Policing the Sampling Strategies

How Earlier Research Has Addressed This Challenge

As noted, a primary concern in these types of surveys is to ensure the sampling strategy was followed and that the enumerator did not exercise discretion in selecting the respondents. I have not been able to find information on how, if at all, compliance with sampling strategies has been policed in previous microenterprise surveys.

My Oversight of Enumerators' Sampling Strategies

Policing the sampling strategy was not simple. I might have randomly sampled textile shop number 3 on the left on the second floor of a given plaza. But, of course, these instructions were imprecise; two enumerators could follow the instructions and end up at different shops if they arrived at the floor using different entrances. But the goal was for the enumerators to *think* that I had preselected a certain shop. When enumerators asked about the multiple entrance issue, I advised them to use the main entrance. Ultimately, however, I was indifferent to which entrance they used, as long as they thought I had preselected the shop.

To audit the sampling strategy, for 10 percent of the surveys I had auditors assess whether the interviewed trader *could have been selected* by following the sampling strategy. Could this shop have *possibly* been the third textile shop from one of the entrances? This was not always straightforward. Sometimes shops are closed, and therefore it is not possible to determine what they are selling. So an enumerator might identify what she perceives to be the third textile shop, while the auditor counts it as the fifth if more shops were open when she visited. I therefore asked auditors to be generous in their assessment. But if the shop did not sell textiles, for example, that indicated a violation of the sampling protocol.

3.2.2 Policing the Survey Administration

The Problem, and How Others Do It
Collecting high-quality survey data is difficult. A number of factors exacerbated the standard hurdles for this survey. First, traders were sometimes distracted by tending to customers during the administration of the survey.[3] Second, I wanted information on sensitive questions. Traders like to present themselves as apolitical and might therefore refuse to answer questions about politics.

Most attempts to police survey administration focus on detecting blatant enumerator fraud. Some researchers run high-frequency checks on the data to ensure the survey was truly conducted. For example, such a check might catch a survey that was administered in just two minutes. Researchers might also conduct audits to ensure the survey was actually conducted.

How I Did It
I used high-frequency checks and audits not only to assess whether the survey was conducted but also to improve data quality. I devised high-frequency checks to draw inferences about how much enumerators were paying attention, how careful they were with number entry, and their ability to elicit truthful responses to sensitive questions. Every night, the field team ran a program on the survey data that generated an Excel sheet with a variety of information. It pulled survey responses that had unrealistically high numbers for responses to questions about the fees traders pay to the market association or trash agency. The program also updated an enumerator's weekly refusal/don't know rate. This showed the percentage of sensitive questions enumerators were not able to elicit responses to. Each morning, the management team met with enumerators about issues raised in the checks with two goals: to ensure the enumerator was more careful, and to clean the survey data.

Sometimes enumerators had kept notes that revealed an extra zero had been entered into the tablet; we used these notes to fix the data. Other times, enumerators returned to a trader to clarify a trader's response. Enumerators who scored badly on a given metric would be assigned to shadow (for a day) an enumerator who excelled in this dimension.

I also conducted back-checks, in which the auditors approached a subset of the surveyed traders. These checks were designed to confirm that the survey was administered, the sampling protocol was followed, the respondent

---

3 No trader wanted to conduct the survey outside business hours.

received the tokens of appreciation, and the respondent felt she was treated with respect. The back-checks also involved asking the respondent eight questions from the survey. For example, the check included a critical question about the trader's main market association. The field management team then compared back-check data to the original survey data, and met with enumerators to retrain them on the question and clean data.

3.3   DEFINING MARKET ASSOCIATION MEMBERSHIP

The Challenge of Identifying Group Membership
The unit of analysis for this project is the market association. I am interested to know which market associations have leaders who represent the interests of traders and which have leaders who extort from their traders. The challenge is that the survey was conducted at the trader level, so I needed to determine which traders belonged to the same association. I am not aware of any other surveys attempting to collect group-level data in this way.

My Approach to Determining Traders' Association Membership
To determine a trader's main business association, I included the following open-ended question in the survey:

What is the main market or plaza association that you belong to?

This question introduced a number of complications. Sometimes traders said they did not belong to any association, but this was rarely the case. Enumerators were trained at the start of the survey, and also retrained periodically during survey implementation on how to follow up on this response. To determine whether the traders did, in fact, belong to an association, the enumerator asked them whether they paid dues to any association, who they paid trash fees to, and whether they attended any meetings. Traders typically *did* belong to an association, but said no at first because they did not have frequent interactions with the market leaders. But it was important to consider these cases as association membership as well. If I missed these cases, the data would be censored to less active associations, which is precisely the important counterfactual that many studies of private groups miss. In some rare cases, traders reported not paying dues or fees to any association and not attending any meetings. I coded this as not belonging to an association. But in most cases, the "no association" response was overcome with a few follow-up questions.

The next challenge was to determine which traders belonged to the same market association so that I could accurately cluster standard errors at the market association level in later analysis. As shown in Table 3.2, this was not always simple.

Imagine trader 1 says their main market association is the Balogun Business Association, and the trader is in a commercial area called Trade Fair. I assign an association ID of 1. Imagine trader 2 belongs to the Balogun Market Association, and is located in Lagos Island. Lagos Island is a different part of the

TABLE 3.2 *Identifying traders who belong to the same market association*

Trader ID	Market name	Area	Association ID
1	Balogun Business Association	Trade Fair	1
2	Balogun Market Association	Lagos Island	2
3	Balogun Trade Association	Lagos Island	2
4	BTA	Lagos Island	2
5	BBA	Trade Fair	1
6	Balogun Trader Union/ Destiny Plaza Association	Lagos Island	Not usable
7	BBA Association in plaza	Trade Fair	3

city, so, despite the similarities in names, this would be a different association, so I assign a new association ID. Then trader 3 reports belonging to the Balogun Trade Association in Lagos Island. Project staff were sent back to trader 3 to ask if the Balogun Trade Association was the same as the Balogun Market Association in Lagos Island. They replied in the affirmative, so this trader was also assigned 2 as the association ID. Several traders, such as traders 4 and 5, provided acronyms, which were usually straightforward to figure out.[4] Occasionally, traders reported belonging to a plaza-level section of a larger association, as trader 7 did. In these cases, project staff were sent back to the trader to ask if the leadership for this chapter was the same as for the broader association. If they were, I assigned the same association ID as the broader association. If they were not, I assigned a unique association ID. Figure 3.3 shows the location of associations represented in the sample.[5]

3.4 MEASURING FRICTIONS TO SORTING

A theme throughout this book is barriers to selecting better-run associations. While in Chapter 7 I discuss differences in these barriers across groups, in Lagos markets, as in many other places, these impediments are substantial. To understand the obstacles to group sorting, the survey asked traders how much rent do they pay for their shop and any "warehouses." Warehouses is the term traders use to reference additional shops they rent out solely to store their goods. These warehouses are typically on upper levels of plazas where customers are unlikely to reach and rent is cheaper. I ask them about rent because of the norms of advance rent, meaning that traders typically pay two

---

4 Sometimes traders gave two associations, such as trader 6 who reported belonging to the Balogun Trader Union and Destiny Plaza Association. I was not able to assign an association ID here, as subsequent questions in the survey were prefilled with the response to this question. For example, a subsequent question asked, "Does [association name prefilled] have an elected leader?" It would not be clear how to interpret a response to this question if two association names were prefilled here. Enumerators were retrained to only write down the respondent's *main* association.
5 Appendix B lists all market associations included in this project.

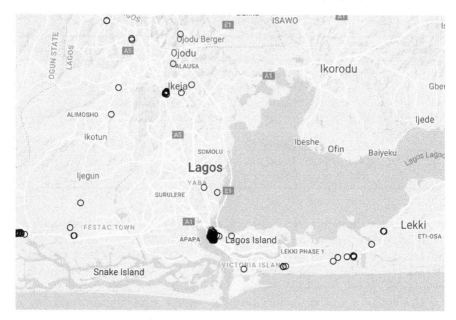

FIGURE 3.3 This is a map of Lagos, with circles plotted at the location of the 199 market associations represented in the survey

years' advance rent to lease a shop. After two years, they need "only" pay one year's advance rent for subsequent years. This disincentivized relocating, as starting over would require cobbling together two full years of rent.

Through my research I have identified strategies future researchers could use to assess hurdles to sorting. Advance rent is a specific example of a startup cost to joining a new group, and better assessing these startup costs qualitatively – for example, by asking for all of the steps involved in switching groups – and quantitatively would be useful. Researchers could also simply ask group members how difficult they think it would be to move. Group members could also be presented with vignettes to assess the conditions under which they would leave their group.

3.5 SUMMARY STATISTICS

Table 3.3 displays trader-level summary statistics based on the survey data. These are relatively sophisticated traders: 77 percent sell at least some whole-sale products, and 81 percent use a smartphone. Traders pay on average $2,126 in annual rent. Remarkably, 54 percent of traders import directly from overseas suppliers (as opposed to buying from a wholesaler based in Nigeria). Yet these are small businesses; the average trader has 0.5 employees. The typical trader in the survey is a 39-year-old Christian man from the Igbo ethnic group.

TABLE 3.3 *Trader-level summary statistics from the 2015 Lagos Trader Survey*

Statistic	N	Mean	St. Dev.	Min	Max
Wholesale	1,010	0.77	0.42	0	1
Smartphone	1,004	0.81	0.39	0	1
Annual rent $	826	2,126	2,107	69.13	29,105
Import	1,010	0.54	0.50	0	1
# employees	1,010	0.50	0.86	0	8
Christian	1,008	0.86	0.35	0	1
Igbo	1,010	0.75	0.43	0	1
Male	1,010	0.73	0.45	0	1
Age	949	38.82	8.85	18	80

I asked traders how their association advocates traders' interests, and then coded their responses. Traders often provided more than one response. They said their association helped to resolve disputes with the local government (14 percent) and among traders in the market (13 percent). According to 14 percent of respondents, their association provides market security. In addition, 8 percent said that their association simply did not advocate for traders, and 12 percent responded by saying "don't know," which might also be interpreted as suggesting the association does not help traders.

In some analyses I leverage data from the second round of the Lagos Trader Survey, conducted in 2016 with 612 of the 1,179 traders from the 2015 survey. Due to budget constraints and the priorities of a separate research project, I aimed to resurvey only traders who imported and a subset of those who sourced goods domestically. I also leverage data from the third round of the Lagos Trader Survey, conducted in 2018 with 834 traders (a 71 percent completion rate). This survey aimed to resurvey all traders from the first round.

I found that association switching is rare. In 2017, just 4 percent of traders were no longer members of the association they belonged to in 2015, suggesting there are real obstacles to leaving associations. When asked why they no longer belonged, traders' responses reflected the nature of living and working in an urban environment and some of the main threats associations face. Some said they relocated to a new plaza. Some alluded to frustration with market governance; one trader said they had joined the association for "price control" benefits, which it failed to deliver. One trader said, "A lot of fraudulent activities are going on in the association, and he can't partake in such [an association] because he is a man of God." Some responses allude to market leadership disputes, which I heard frequently during my fieldwork: one trader said their prior association no longer controls the plaza, and another said the association fell apart after a "power tussle." Some alluded to the renovation of their market, noting that the building they traded out of in 2015 was destroyed and the association did not persist through the construction of the new building. And lastly, one trader said they did not belong to the association anymore because "the leader suddenly left her position saying she doesn't want to die early and since then nobody wants to be the leader so the association was dissolved." In the 2018 survey, 7 percent reported no longer belonging to the association they were a member of in either 2015 or 2016, depending on when they were last surveyed.

I found that there was variation in whether traders changed the product they sold over the years. Of the traders selling apparel in 2015, 88 percent also sold apparel in 2016 and 2018. Traders selling electronics had similarly high rates of staying with that product. But of traders selling home goods in 2015, only 29 percent reported selling home goods in both 2016 and 2018. The rates of sticking with hardware and beauty items over the four-year period were more moderate, at 59 percent and 36 percent, respectively. The reason for this variation is unclear. During the course of the panel, Nigeria experienced a financial crisis that weakened the local currency. This made it more difficult for traders to import or to purchase imported products. But it is not obvious how this would differentially affect traders; products in all of these categories are imported. One possibility is that apparel and electronics are more capital-intensive; traders selling these products may be wealthier and have more of a cushion to withstand financial shocks.

3.6 CONCLUSION

In this chapter I detailed how I created a sample frame of informal traders, sampled from that census, and matched each trader with an association. My techniques made the survey more representative than prior surveys of similar populations. For example, my surveys included markets on the outskirts of the city, which previous studies have typically ignored. I also audited the survey as well as the sampling strategy. This is rarely done, but it is important because it reduces the opportunities for enumerator discretion, which can lead them to approach traders who are systematically different. In Chapter 5 I use a combination of random and convenience sampling with the survey data to select four market case studies for more in-depth investigation. In Chapter 6 I use the survey data to test several implications of my argument.

If future firm surveys identify associational membership, these studies could consider how group affiliation impacts firm growth. Associations shape firms' day-to-day experiences; they can prevent government extortion, or not. Group leaders can themselves extort, or not. Associations may be as important for explaining growth as the variables economists typically focus on, such as business training and access to capital. While some surveys ask whether a trader belongs to an association – yes or no – that information is unhelpful without related data on the association's attributes. This chapter has introduced strategies to collect this information; these strategies will improve the ability of future surveys to identify barriers to trade.

Studies of firm growth depend on accurately estimating firm size. My strategy for auditing the sampling protocol will improve these estimates. Many sampling strategies would in practice permit an enumerator to violate the sampling protocol and approach an idle trader. These traders will be easier to interview, but this type of error will lead to downward bias due to firm size, as busier traders fare better. Additionally, larger firms are more likely to have employees, and the owner – the individual who most studies want to survey – will be less likely to be at the shop. This will be especially likely if the owner has more than one shop. For smaller firms, it will be easier for enumerators to conduct the interview on the first visit as the owner is more likely to be present. This error will also downward bias firm size. It is possible that developing country firms are larger than we think because of these types of sampling errors.

Specific survey questions can also help researchers estimate firm size. I asked traders how many additional shops they had, and the average trader had 0.24 other shops. Subsequent questions about revenue, for example, referenced *all* of a trader's shops. Failing to account for multiple shops could also result in underestimating firm size.

Additionally, in administering this survey, I was alerted to a distinct attribute of the traders. To avoid taxes and stay profitable during economic downturns, two or more traders may share one physical space. One does not work for the other, and they are not co-owners; they have separate businesses in the same small shop. In research for more recent projects, I therefore include a question in the survey that asks traders whether they share their shop with any other trader(s), and, if so, how many. I then seek to interview all shop sharers for every trader sampled. While the strategies outlined in this chapter address many biases in existing surveys that result in sampling fewer small businesses, going forward, accounting for shop sharing will further address this matter.

I struggled to obtain a list of Lagos market *associations*, so I started with the second-best option: a list of *markets* from the Lagos trash agency. This strategy could be even more useful for other surveys. Government entities elsewhere may keep lists of informal associations. For example, a local government or a political party may have a list of neighborhood associations. In Lagos, though the Ministry of Commerce and Industry did not have a list of market associations, they did manage a list of trade associations, with contact information for each. These lists could make the job of other researchers easier than mine was here. Starting with a list of associations allows respondents to be stratified by association and avoids the time-consuming task of determining who belongs to each association.

Even if a researcher obtains an accurate list of the universe of associations, the challenges discussed in this chapter about the trader-level census are generalizable. Lagos market associations are not the only type of group that has incentives to misrepresent its size. While market associations understate membership numbers to avoid taxes, neighborhood associations may overstate their membership to appear more politically important. If my census strategy was workable in the biggest city in Africa among tens of thousands of traders, it should be feasible for poor neighborhoods or other market contexts. The approach may be less useful, however, for associations comprised of members who lack obvious physical locations, like an association of hairstylists, who often work out of their homes. It may not be possible – even with limitless resources – to find all members of this group by brute force. In these cases, researchers may need to work with associations and consider how to align researcher and association goals.

Lastly, this chapter highlighted the importance of taking word choice seriously. Taking the time to figure out how individuals talk about their group matters. What do people call their group? A union? Or "the executives"? What language do they use to describe desirable and undesirable group leader behavior? Using uncommon language could lead researchers to understate the importance of associations in people's lives.

4

A Calm Sea Does not Make a Good Sailor: A Theory of Private Good Governance

Economic actors have evolved in different ways to deal with contracting problems (Dixit, 2004). Firms can structure themselves in ways that minimize exposure to opportunistic behavior with diversified business groups (Ghemawat and Khanna, 1998; Leff, 1978; Post, 2014) and vertical integration (Williamson, 1971). Likewise, firms can opt into relational contracts (Macneil, 1977). The prospect of punishment in public courts can constrain cheating.

Arms-length, impersonal trade, however, can exist even in contexts where the state does not protect property or enforce contracts, even when vertical integration is not feasible, and even if there are many obstacles to relational contracting. Private groups can police the behavior of their members by punishing dishonest actions; they can also incentivize information sharing about unreliable traders outside the group and organize boycotts of those who cheat group members. The efficiency gains that such groups can secure, however, do not guarantee that they will emerge.

A theory of private good governance should not just describe institutions that support trade.[1] It should also outline hurdles to the emergence of these institutions and explain how these hurdles will be overcome. In this chapter I attempt to do exactly that. I start by presenting two broad critiques of the private governance literature. First, this research sometimes assumes that groups can self-regulate without group leaders. While this might be the case for some small groups, leaders are critical for cooperation in many groups. Second, scholars have overlooked the obstacles group leaders must overcome in order to govern well – such as impediments to truthful information sharing and impartial dispute enforcement – which has generated the faulty assumption that private order will emerge when it is needed.

---

[1] A variety of terms are used across literatures to reference the outcome studied here. Private governance, self-governance, self-regulation, and private ordering all reference the extent to which a group promotes behavior that furthers the interests of the group as a whole. These terms can be used to describe either leader behavior or cases in which group members cooperate in the absence of a leader. I use these terms interchangeably.

I then develop the logic of my argument, which expands our understanding of the conditions that make private trade-promoting policies more likely. While previous studies of private groups suggest that private institutions *substitute for* public institutions (e.g., Greif, 1993; Richman, 2006), I argue that state threats can encourage private good governance and render it more important; private associations will predate without public institutions that force them to behave otherwise. To my knowledge, I am also the first to show that public officials need not be benevolent to motivate private good governance. My argument is consistent with previous work on how private groups function, but focuses on the less understood dimension of why private good governance does not always emerge when it is needed.

4.1   CRITIQUES OF LITERATURE

There is a consensus across a vast interdisciplinary theoretical and empirical literature that enforcement and information-sharing institutions enable trade. My critique of this body of research takes two forms. First, these studies often suggest that enforcement and information sharing can occur without leaders. I argue that the scope conditions necessary for this to take place are quite narrow. Second, research on private governance stops at proximate explanations.

4.1.1   Implicit Suggestions of Self-Regulation without Leaders

Research in the fields of political science, economics, and law and economics has focused on groups in which the collective punishment of (and information sharing about) dishonest individuals occurs organically. I agree that such groups exist. However, this work often implies that self-regulation without leaders is common, and that it will emerge when needed, which I do not believe to be the case. Organic self-regulation is most likely only in relatively small groups, and even then it cannot be assumed.

Robert Ellickson's well-known book *Order Without Law* is among the more prominent works to selectively choose cases in this way (1991). Ellickson observed high levels of cooperation among ranchers in Shasta County, California, in the 1970s. There were widely accepted norms regarding appropriate behavior related to animal trespassing, and deviations from these norms were rare. When ranchers (typically newcomers) engaged in opportunistic behavior, "self-help retaliation" occurred in the form of "truthful negative gossip" (p. 57). But what prevented false negative gossip designed to besmirch a newcomer's reputation (Duggan, Forthcoming)? No real explanation is given beyond the suggestion that people care about being good neighbors. If there is indeed little false gossip, which is possible, this merits an explanation. What makes this group so cohesive? The situation described in Shasta County is unlikely to be the norm in rural America, yet Ellickson concludes from this study that "order often arises spontaneously" (p. 4).

Ellickson is taking on the Coase theorem, which holds that, when there are no transaction costs, market forces will produce an optimal resource allocation: parties will bargain from their legally established entitlements. However, his interpretation of the theorem is misguided. Ellickson argues persuasively that the Shasta County ranchers were unfamiliar with the subtleties of the laws regulating their business, and thus bargained based on their own norms of cooperation. As Ingleby (1994) has noted, though, this interpretation is based on a narrow definition of the law. Law, for example, created the boundaries of Shasta County and thus provided a clear demarcation for a community to decide who the norms of cooperation apply to (Brigham and Ellickson, 1993), a condition that Ostrom (1990) has noted is important for private governance. And Ellickson himself acknowledges the role of county authorities in backstopping cooperative behavior. Ingleby notes: "Conclusions such as that '[t]he expense of consulting lawyers makes going to law a negative-sum game' (p. 274) or that '[i]n many contexts, law is not central to the maintenance of social order' (p. 280), only make sense if one limits one's definition of law to rules which govern the resolution of disputes" (1994, p. 331).

Order Without Law is not the only work to focus on cases in which truthful reputational information spreads organically, and pay little attention to how this happens when individuals are in competition with each other and have many incentives to falsely hurt their competitors' reputations. For example, Edward Stringham has written a series of papers on private contract enforcement in early European stock exchanges (2003; 2002). He argues that trader reputations simply became known and describes a system in which individuals who defaulted had their names written on blackboards for all to see (2003, p. 5). Yet he neglects to explain who wrote these names and does not discuss the wronged party's incentives to reveal the identity of the cheater. This is not to dispute the empirics. Rather, the framing of this literature implies that, in the absence of state enforcement of contracts, useful information will organically reach those who need it. But – with some exceptions, notably Richman (2017) and Skarbek (2014) – past works overlook *how this comes about*: ignoring the obstacles to truthful reputational systems implies that these systems will simply emerge whenever they are needed.

The ethnic politics literature on occasion similarly implies that self-regulation without leaders can be assumed. Studies on the connection between politics and ethnicity frequently argue that ethnic groups are better placed to sanction in-group defectors than out-group members. Fearon and Laitin (1996) describe an equilibrium in which interethnic cooperation is maintained by having in-group members sanction their own for cheating out-group members. In-group members have informational advantages: if a group member cheats someone from a different group, other members of the group are best placed to identify the opportunist, given the denser social networks.

However, the ethnic politics literature misses two key points. First, members of trading communities may be in competition with each other. Just because they are connected to other group members does not imply that information will effortlessly spread. Second, Fearon and Laitin's argument is that – assuming there is not too much noise – individual group members will sanction each other; they do not discuss leaders. But in the real world, there is a lot of noise. Leaders are needed to dig through this noise and assess culpability. As McMillan and Woodruff note, "private order, if it is to operate at all, needs to be *organized*" (2000, p. 2423).

Recent work from the urban politics literature provides helpful portraits of informal group leaders in cities that informs my approach to theorizing about these leaders. Jeffrey Paller (2019), for example, examines how leader and group attributes and political incentives interact to influence slum leader conduct in urban Ghana. Adam Auerbach and Tariq Thachil investigate which traits slum residents value when selecting community leaders (2018). Barnes (2017) studies how state presence and intergang competition change how gang leaders treat group members. These studies demonstrate the relevance of leaders and describe them as complicated individuals who can behave in many different ways.

4.1.2   Under-Theorized Hurdles to Self-Regulation

Not all research assumes that truthful information will quickly spread to the people who need it. Larson (2017) challenges assumptions that information will organically spread within groups, and considers the effect of hurdles to information sharing on in-group sanctioning. My contribution is to focus on leader (rather than peer) sanctioning and highlight the additional hurdles to information sharing that arise in a competitive trading context.

Similarly, not all research assumes that the prospect of group shaming is sufficient to deter opportunistic behavior. Many studies have examined the sophisticated institutions found in groups that engage in effective private governance (e.g., Milgrom, North and Weingast, 1990; Richman, 2017; Skarbek, 2014). I agree with the emphasis this research places on information sharing and enforcement institutions in promoting trade. The explanations of these institutions, however, are sometimes proximate, and ignoring cases of unsuccessful governance inhibits the study of successful private governance.

I use Ostrom's eight "design principles" associated with successful self-governance (1990) as a starting point for my analysis. For Ostrom, successful self-governance depends on features such as clear group boundaries, the ability of community members to participate in rule modification, graduated sanctions for rule violators, and low-cost strategies for dispute resolution.

The logical next step is to ask how these principles come about, and my book attempts to answer that question. Who decides when to implement these sanctions? Who adjudicates disputes to decide when (and which) sanctions are appropriate? Who will provide accessible dispute-resolution services? What will prevent group leaders from using this power to advance their personal interests?

In other work, Ostrom highlights resource and user attributes that make institutional arrangements sustainable (Ostrom, 2005, p. 1). For example, resource users must trust each other. But this requirement is itself endogenous to private governance. Intragroup trust partly depends on whether group leaders create conditions that enable trust, or whether they sow distrust within a group.

Further, what prevents group leaders from simply extorting from their members? Under what conditions are group leaders incentivized to serve interests outside their own? When a group leader could punish an opportunistic group member for cheating an outsider, what prevents the leader from accepting a bribe from the member to not enforce the punishment? The literature leaves such important questions unanswered. A few studies have touched on private constitutions and internal systems of checks and balances (e.g., Leeson, 2007). For example, Skarbek observes that American prison gang constitutions have sophisticated provisions to check gang leader power, such as rules for impeachment (Skarbek, 2014, p. 126). But these explanations are incomplete. What limits internal collusion? What constrains a predatory leader from using the powers of incumbency to buy off or slander those who oppose his or her rule? Indeed, Skarbek documents an instance when these provisions failed to dissuade leader embezzlement (Skarbek, 2014, p. 126).[2]

Lisa Bernstein and Barak Richman examine private ordering in the diamond industry, in which a desire for secrecy discourages the use of formal, legally enforceable contracts (Bernstein, 1992, 2001; Richman, 2017). They describe how the New York Diamond Dealers Club (DDC) trade association provides private dispute adjudication and disseminates information about individuals who do not abide by arbitration rulings. A superficial look at the diamond trade might suggest that information sharing occurs organically, since the industry is based in a close-knit Orthodox Jewish community and members can exchange information on a physical message board if they feel their reputation is being unfairly maligned. Both authors highlight, however, that leaders play an important role in information sharing. The DDC arbitrates disputes and posts information on the message board about members who do not comply with a ruling (1992, p. 128). Diamond traders will not easily share information with competitors: one trader notes that he will share information only with those close to him (Richman, 2017, pp. 47–48). Bernstein's study overlooks the *origins* of effective private governance, and she acknowledges that the diamond industry has a *uniquely* effective private governance system. Richman's work raises questions about the factors that support DDC leadership activities. He notes that a DDC arbitration board can independently punish individuals for sharing false information (Richman, 2017, p. 46). But how would the board identify such falsehoods and recognize them as untrue?

[2] The business association literature explores the attributes of successful business associations and finds that developing states need close cooperation with business associations in order to pursue economic growth, but the state must be able to act on its own independent interests (Evans, 1995). This argument, though, tells us little about the conditions under which localized growth would be observed in developing states. Business associations that self-police in developing states are theorized to promote development (Maxfield and Schneider, 1997), but it is not clear why some associations self-police, while others do not. Likewise, the literature has focused on clustering – firms with sectoral and spatial concentration – but has largely neglected comparisons of clusters with more dispersed firms (Schmitz and Nadvi, 1999).

This is not to deny their abilities, but just to note that the costs to leaders of engaging in such work must be enormous, and it is unclear what incentivizes them to act in such a way.

A body of work that spans both development economics and law and economics similarly considers the relationship between public and private enforcement institutions – in particular, whether public institutions crowd out or complement their private counterparts (e.g., McMillan and Woodruff, 2000). However, the literature does not explain variation in the presence of private good governance institutions across groups with similar access to public institutions. It instead compares the efficiency gains of private versus public ordering, and sometimes assumes that the order that most effectively minimizes the transaction costs will be available (Richman, 2004).

In short, prior research on private governance focuses on groups that have sophisticated private institutions (i.e., rules of the game) that promote trade. Scholars focus on *describing* these institutions and detailing *how* they promote trade. While some studies do discuss the very real challenges to self-governance (e.g., group member cooptation (Keshavarzian, 2007)), much of this work ignores both badly governed groups and the costs to group leaders of providing trade-promoting policies, and instead implies that trade-promoting private groups will emerge to fill gaps in the public provision of social order. In fact, such groups are exceptional. Badly governed groups abound; they simply do not attract scholars' attention. The myth of spontaneous order overlooks the standard collective action hurdles to the provision of private pro-trade policies (Bates, 1988). Weingast et al. (2013) theorize about the costs to individuals of complying with collective punishment, but coordination also entails costs to leaders. Leaders must sometimes go against the short-term interests of group members, and it is costly – in terms of time, money, and reputation – to determine culpability and monitor compliance with collective punishment. Even the highly effective DDC struggles with these challenges; critics maintain that its arbitration system is biased in favor of DDC members (Richman, 2017). Later, I propose an explanation of the conditions under which private leaders are more likely to overcome these hurdles.

4.2 PROVISION OF PRIVATE TRADE-PROMOTING POLICIES

When will group leaders implement trade-promoting policies?[3] I argue that government threats can motivate group leaders to act in the long-term interests of their members. Government threats will be more likely to have this

---

[3] I use the term leader to refer to the individual (or individuals) who governs a group. Other studies might use the term association or organization, but I avoid those terms, when possible, to avoid confusing the people who head the group with the group as a whole. I use the term policy to reference leaders' specific actions. I mostly avoid the term institution, which could refer to either a specific market association or its "rules of the game" (North, 1993). To avoid conflating these terms, I will use group, group leader, and policies. When I do use the term institution, it will be to refer to the "rules of the game."

effect when group leaders can control the internal affairs of their group and when group members do *not* compete with each other. Under these conditions, an equilibrium can emerge in which group leaders act in the interests of their members in order to retain the ability to mobilize them politically – for example, through protest – against government threats. Group leaders will feel freer to extort from members when member support matters less.

What, concretely, are these trade-promoting policies? Successful private governance results in the provision of two critical local public goods.[4] The first is the provision of neutral dispute-resolution services, both between group members, and between group members and non-group members. For many groups, dispute resolution is analogous to private contract enforcement: group leaders mediate disputes about the terms of a verbal or written contract. I use the terms dispute-resolution services and enforcement institutions interchangeably to refer to this service. The consistent, impartial provision of dispute-adjudication services is a reputational local public good: if outsiders feel comfortable doing business with the group, group members will benefit since outsiders will be more likely to trade with them. If a dispute between an outsider and a group member arises, the outsider should be able to trust the group leader to mediate impartially. The second key local public good is information sharing. Leaders can share different types of information that promotes trade, such as the identity of dishonest outsiders with whom group members should avoid engaging.

Successful private governance also results in an absence of private extortion, which I define as a situation in which group leaders collect fees from members that are not used in promoting the interests of the group. Group members often have a good sense of whether their leaders properly account for how they spend group taxes.

I take the organizational form as exogenous, focusing on groups that have leaders, which is largely the case for informal groups around the world (e.g., Auerbach, 2017), and in virtually all of the markets studied here.[5] The argument applies to contexts in which group members cannot rely on public institutions to impartially and efficiently enforce contracts and protect property rights, such as trade associations in countries with unclear laws where public institutions unevenly and inefficiently enforce agreements. In particular, the theory applies in cities, where individuals may be more mobile and less socially embedded in the lives of their fellow group members. Embeddedness – particularly in rural communities – can constrain opportunism. In its absence, I expect the role of state threats to be more pronounced.

---

[4] These are also called club goods.

[5] I use the term informality to reference trade that is conducted by businesses that are not registered with all relevant government entities, or transactions that are not formally documented. This term is relevant, as it affects whether firms can rely on public institutions to enforce contracts and protect property. Conventional use of the term informal trade may suggest that it is untaxed, but this need not be the case. Indeed, local authorities all over the world frequently tax informal trade, both legally and illegally.

4.2.1 Incentives

To explain the presence or absence of these pro-trade policies, we need to first understand the incentives of three actors. My theory centers on two main actors: group leaders and politicians. The third actor, traders (group members), plays a secondary role.

The argument focuses on contexts in which group leaders are members of (and elected by) the group. I assume they are self-interested and aim to maximize their personal wealth by collecting fees from traders, which are roughly proportional to group profits. Group leaders have varying time horizons that may impact the extent to which their goals align with those of the group's members, depending on whether their position is subject to terms and term limits, or (less commonly) on whether it is a lifetime appointment.

Group leadership provides a number of opportunities to accumulate wealth. Of course, a leader could collect and pocket high fees from traders. But he or she can also acquire respect, connections, and social status, which could be monetized at a later date. A leader could also collect fees for resolving disputes in the market – either in a predatory or in a fair manner. For these reasons, leaders will want to maintain their formal title as well as their de facto ability to control affairs in the market.

I assume group leaders have the right to sanction group members, though they may not always choose to, and may do so without cause. There are costs associated with fair sanctioning – for example, the time and resources required to determine who is in the wrong in a dispute.

Both elected and unelected government officials can threaten markets. I focus on local elected politicians. I assume they have terms and term limits, and that they seek higher government positions. To climb the party ranks, they must increase the internally generated revenue and maintain voter support. I assume that certain characteristics of the groups under their jurisdiction constrain their ability to collect revenue, including the type of land the market is on and the market association's degree of political power.

Government bureaucrats and police will similarly face diverse incentives, though most will aim to keep their job. This requires balancing the needs of their supervisors (who may pressure them to raise revenue) with placating powerful societal groups. As Olly Owen has written about the Nigerian police, "mishandling a matter involving a sensitive social group [...] can bring unexpected and swift career reversal" (2017).

In trade groups, group members may or may not compete with each other, depending on whether they sell the same products or services. When in competition, members will be more reluctant to share valuable trade information, and general cooperation will be harder to achieve.

My argument rests on the assumption that group members aim to maximize their income, which partly depends on whether they are part of a group that has pro-trade policies. However, group members may have imperfect information about group conditions prior to joining, and they may also have imperfect information about the conditions in other groups, which constrains their ability to make comparisons. Once they are part of a group, even with perfect information, frictions may prevent them from switching to a better group.[6]

These characteristics apply to many informal groups. For example, in Indian slums, among the overwhelming majority who acknowledge the existence of informal leadership, more than half reported that their leaders came to power through informal elections or community meetings (Auerbach and Thachil, 2018). Likewise, residents of Rio de Janeiro's favelas elect neighborhood association leaders (Gay, 2010), and bus owners elect leaders of the Uganda Taxi Operators and Drivers Association (Goodfellow, 2016). Private fee collection occurs across all of these informal associations. Group switching is similarly challenging in poor neighborhoods, or when there is only one transport association.

4.2.2 Strong and Weak Leaders

There are two types of group leaders: strong and weak ones. Building on Peter Leeson's emphasis on leader strength (2014), I propose that strong leaders can control the group's internal affairs and have the de facto right to adjudicate disputes that occur within the group. They have the ability to spread information quickly within the group and to punish group members. Strong leaders can use their strength either to predate on members or to implement trade-promoting policies.

Weak leaders cannot control internal group affairs. They may try to call a meeting to share information, but many members will not attend. Likewise, members may not bring within-group disputes to a weak leader and may not pay fines imposed by a leader who lacks control.

Why, then, are some market leaders strong and others weak? I lacked strong priors on this question, but I broadly expected leader strength to be a function of both systematic and idiosyncratic factors. Long-standing norms may determine whether members comply with leader policies, and whether a leader can conditionally provide or withhold valuable services matters. Divisions within a group may be so salient and so long-standing that no leader can earn the respect and compliance of all traders. In rare instances, a leader's ties to thugs might help the leader ensure group compliance. Market case studies in Chapter 5 inductively generate ideas about the determinants of leader strength. I did, however, expect leader strength to be persistent over time, as theory-generating conversations had suggested as much.

The key point is that market leader strength is distinct from *how they use that strength*. Strong leaders, for example, can use their strength either to impartially resolve disputes or to accept a bribe from a disputant to side with them.

4.2.3 Government Threats

The state can shape private governance in several ways. For example, it can directly provide services like contract enforcement and property rights

---

[6] Section 4.7 discusses these frictions.

protection, obviating the need for private institutions. Or the state can provide services that enable private good governance. For example, public officials can offset the costs of common resource governance by assisting with resource use monitoring (Ostrom, 1990). The state can also provide residents with ID cards, which can help group leaders ascertain the identity of individuals who wish to trade with group members.

I introduce a new way in which the state can motivate private good governance: by threatening to intervene in the group's functioning in a way that the group perceives as predatory. I conceptualize threats from elected politicians and appointed government officials similarly, since threats of intervention from either could motivate leader responsiveness. Group mobilization can constrain appointed officials and bureaucrats as well as elected officials, as the former are accountable to the latter.

Charles Tilly argues that modern states developed in Europe in response to external hostility; states were forced to respond to civilian preferences because they needed civilian support – in the form of money and labor – for survival (1992). I extend his argument to private actors.

What state threats could private groups encounter? Politicians who wish to modernize their community might aim to demolish and rebuild a market. Likewise, they could threaten to increase taxes or rent. Regulatory agencies or the police could impose fines or lock up shops. Groups without physical marketplaces would face similar threats. For example, government officials could rescind the licenses of an association for furniture manufacturers or threaten to impose new regulations or fees.

These threats can jeopardize traders' livelihoods, since a police presence can scare the customers away. Since market leaders are also traders and usually have substantial businesses, these threats would affect them as well. If traders are asked to pay additional fees to a government agency, the market leader might be forced to accept delayed or lowered payments. In some instances, the threat might challenge the market leader's control over the market.

Other threats emanating from private actors, such as organized criminal groups, or global forces, such as an increase in the price of a commodity, are also salient. I am ambivalent as to how these threats will shape groups, as Barnes has found that non-state threats affect group leaders' incentives differently than state threats (2017). Empirically, however, the majority of threats that trade organizations face come from government actors, and so I focus on those threats.

Why do some groups face government threats, while others do not? Some neighborhoods or markets may be located on land that makes them more vulnerable to demolition. Some groups might be under the jurisdiction of a more activist local government. A change in political leadership may lead to threats against a group where there were none before. Groups selling or making certain products might have more interactions with a specific interventionist regulatory agency.

One concern for the theory is that well-governed groups may also be more prosperous, and that this may attract local government attention and threats to the group. This is a difficult possibility to address empirically, as I expect well-governed groups to be run by strong leaders, who, in turn, should be better able to negotiate with local politicians, which makes it difficult to observe threats toward these markets in equilibrium. However, I do not expect good governance of a group to cause massive increases in group prosperity. For example, if the leadership of a furniture manufacturing association suddenly improved dramatically, this would have only a modest impact on profits. If the leader started punishing manufacturers who cut corners and used wood that warped easily, for instance, customers would put more faith in furniture made by members of this association over time and start to buy more furniture. This could increase manufacturer profits somewhat, but when businesses are small – which they are in developing countries for many reasons that are beyond the scope of this project – there are limits on expansion. The difference in the volume of trade between two furniture associations, each with fifty members, and one with a leader who enforces quality rules, would not be so substantial that politicians would ignore one and focus on the other.

4.2.4 Group Leader Threats

Strong leaders who refrain from predating on group members can mobilize members to deter state intervention in a number of ways. For example, politicians may want to signal to patrons that they have the support of organized societal groups. If a group mobilizes as a bloc to vote against a politician or protest, this is a credible signal of discontent – even if the group is not that large. Similarly, a group can engage in credible acts of approval, for instance, by rallying in favor of a politician.

Facing the prospect of government intrusion, strong leaders will take other productive steps in addition to restraining from extorting. Disputes between group members and outsiders can provide an opportunity for government officials to involve themselves in group affairs. To prevent such an intervention, which may involve collecting fees and scaring away customers, leaders will be more likely to (1) spread information to group members about dubious outsiders to avoid trading with and (2) impartially resolve disputes. Acquiring information about fraudsters is costly, and group members are motivated to keep this information to themselves to prevent giving their competitors an advantage. Leaders can acquire valuable information about who is (and is not) trustworthy by resolving disputes. Strong leaders can also organize boycotts of fraudsters, which would involve punishing group members for trading with an individual who had been boycotted. But this is similarly tricky: leaders must identify and punish traders who break the boycott.

I build on the consensus that leader strength matters by explaining the conditions under which strength will or will not be used to predate on group members. I argue that, when a leader is strong and faces threats from politicians, he or she will be less likely to extort. This will allow the leader to mobilize traders to deter state intervention. If a leader extorts, they will alienate the traders and be unable to motivate them to vote for a preferred candidate.

Nor will the leader be able to motivate traders to, for example, spend a Saturday protesting against a politician. To deter government intrusion in the group, strong leaders will take action to limit disputes. For example, they will be more likely to acquire and share information with traders about fraudsters and help traders resolve disputes.

Could leaders extort from group members while also promoting trade? I expect members to accept leaders pocketing some portion of the fees collected in exchange for the time they devote to running the group. But by definition, extortion or predatory fee collection is inconsistent with good governance, as it amounts to unfair fee collection.

Even if leaders are elected with a majority of votes, they may not necessarily have sufficient support to mobilize group members *as a whole*; this requires broad and deep support. For example, the most powerful signal a market can send to politicians is to shut down for a day and protest or rally. These forms of mobilization are credible and threatening to politicians because they are costly for traders, who must support the leader's vision sufficiently to forgo a day's revenue in the market. Politicians will be less worried about protesting by a small contingent from the market; meaningful threats require comprehensive group support.

4.3 COMPETITION

Threats will not always lead to private good governance. I expect that, when group members compete with each other, it will be harder for leaders to elicit information about dishonest trading partners. It will also be harder to promote group cooperation of any sort, including protest efforts. I therefore expect high levels of intragroup competition to frustrate group leader efforts to support trade. What might competition look like? Banks compete for creditworthy loan applicants. Tailors compete for clients. Wholesale traders compete for purchases from retailers.

How does competition shape incentives to share information? On the one hand, an individual may want competitors to be aware of, for example, their opportunistic supplier. The prospect of information about uncooperative behavior spreading can incentivize cooperative behavior; suppliers will be less likely to cheat if they know many potential buyers will learn of their behavior. On the other hand, if there are simply "bad" types and "good" types, and deterrent effects are irrelevant, information sharing could hurt one's competitive advantage. Why would an individual want a competitor to learn the identity of their best (or worst) supplier?

Firms are aware of these competing incentives. Banks, for example, carefully calculate the costs and benefits of participating in a credit bureau. The benefits are clear: they would gain information about loan applicant track records, along with the deterrent effect that borrowers fear that information about a loan default will be shared with other banks. But there are also costs: other banks will benefit from its currently private information about individual creditworthiness (Padilla and Pagano, 1997).

Cooperation is possible in the presence of competition – after all, credit bureaus exist – but competition exacerbates free-riding problems and makes cooperation harder to sustain. Research suggests that joint ventures are less likely to succeed when the partners are direct competitors (Park and Russo, 1996). In an experimental study, Hardy and McCasland (2016) showed that tailors respond to the rival nature of demand when assessing whether to teach another tailor a new design. Experimental evidence from China shows that firms are less likely to share information when they are in competition with each other (Cai and Szeidl, 2017).

Credit bureaus cleverly motivate cooperation by withholding valuable information unless a bank shares information about its own customers. In the medieval Champagne fairs, a different mechanism incentivized information sharing – an effective dispute-resolution service. If a trader wanted help resolving a dispute, a centralized judge required information about the offending party, which the judge could then share with others.

While several studies have explored the technical ways in which communication is costly (Milgrom, North and Weingast, 1990), the effects of competition on information sharing have been largely overlooked. Yet these effects are arguably at least as important since they raise the hurdles to private good governance.

4.4 CORE PREDICTIONS

The following testable predictions emerge from this discussion:

1. Market leaders who govern markets that face state threats will be less likely to extort and more likely to invest in other pro-trade policies than those in charge of markets that face fewer state threats. This relationship should be greater when traders are *not* in competition with each other.
2. Market leaders' political engagement should be associated with less private extortion and the presence of other trade-promoting policies.

4.5 COLLUSION

The possibility of leader–politician collusion complicates the argument presented here, which assumes that, when strong group leaders are confronted with meddling politicians, the leaders will be motivated to take actions in the interest of group members. But what if the leader instead colludes with the politician?

Empirically, such collusion is rare in Lagos markets. Traders report collusion in just 14 percent of the markets.[7] In the chapters that follow, I largely ignore the possibility of collusion for this reason.

---

[7] Data from the 2016 survey. Given the possibility that traders were reluctant to report collusion, I assume that, if just one trader reported that their market leader had ever colluded, then this is probably true – even if none of the other traders revealed this.

Why is collusion rare in Lagos market associations? First, while a local politician stands to benefit from higher taxes collected by colluding with a market association leader – after all, the leader has better information about the volume of trade and often more power – the group leader has less to gain from such an arrangement. The leader likely already has detailed information about the volume of trade in the market, and it is not clear how the politician would be able to help the leader extract further revenue. Second, there are substantial costs associated with entering into a collusive arrangement. In particular, colluding parties must develop sophisticated monitoring strategies to detect defections – for example, a leader underreporting collected fees to a local politician (Ivaldi et al., 2007). This information would be very difficult for the politician to collect. Leaders have high levels of information about conditions and happenings in their group, which would be hard for outsiders to obtain. The hurdles to these strategies are substantial for group leaders and politicians, especially when local politician turnover is high. Moreover, these factors are not unique to Lagos markets. Private group leaders often have great power over the group and little to gain from working with a politician, and it is unclear how the development of monitoring institutions would be easier elsewhere.

In the rare instances where I observe market leaders colluding with politicians in survey data, it is because the government could somehow help the market leader extort from the traders (35 percent of traders who reported that their market leader had colluded gave this reason), or because the market leader was at imminent risk of losing their position and the collusion helped reassert control over the traders (9 percent gave this reason).[8] One trader said the leaders colluded "to assert their superiority over the traders." Another said the market leader had colluded to "overrule the market laws and rules guiding us."

Throughout the year of fieldwork, I witnessed only one market that colluded with a local politician. This case supports the control motivation, as the market leader colluded with a local politician to maintain his leadership position. In this market, the leader had been extraordinarily predatory and had recently modified the association's constitution in such a way that suppressed opposition. This infuriated traders, who were working to overthrow him – a rare endeavor. The leader colluded with the local government – facilitating its effort to renovate the market to the perceived detriment of traders – in exchange for the local government backing his claim to the leadership position.

Theoretically, this account is logical. In the absence of an imminent loss of power, market executives would have little to gain from conspiring with local politicians. Except in unusual circumstances, market executives in this context have autonomy, an informational advantage over politicians, and greater authority to collect fees. The gains for a market leader of collusion will rarely exceed the costs unless his or her position is at stake. While it is possible that

---

[8] The remaining responses were ambiguous.

the threat of collective anger could constrain collusion, in this case it occurred when collective anger was at its highest: when the leader feared losing his position. Collusion emerged as the only option to maintain power.

4.6 RELATIONAL CONTRACTING

This book is about the conditions under which group leaders invest in policies to support trade where legal institutions are weak or biased. Some may counter that such policies are not needed, as relational contracting is sufficient to enable trade. Relational contracting is an informal system in which the prospect of future trade promotes honest behavior among traders. Such transactional relationships are characterized by incompletely specified agreements and a willingness to continually renegotiate (Gibbons and Henderson, 2012). But conversations with traders and analysis of novel transaction-level data suggest that, under many conditions, long-term relationships between trading partners do not guarantee honest behavior.

For instance, the owner of a small shop had bought for many years his canned beans from the same local wholesaler, who frequently mixed expired cans in with the order. For some reason, this long-term relationship did not motivate honest behavior. The survey data show similar dynamics. Based on data from 3,911 import purchases in the 2015 survey data, for every additional year two individuals have been trading with each other, the importer is just 0.1 percent less likely to report receiving defective products. The likelihood of receiving defective products remains fairly high until trading relationships exceed fifteen years.[9]

I propose that long-term relationships do not solve contracting problems for four reasons. First, two traders may have incomplete information about the structure of the game they are playing. For example, unpredictable political environments can make it difficult to assess how much a trading partner will gain from future trade (Biggs and Shah, 2006). Traders may also have private information about shocks to their environment. For instance, a winemaker may have private information about local weather conditions and how the weather affected the harvest. It can be hard to hide information about such shocks when two traders are in neighboring rural villages. But in dense urban environments, and particularly when traders in the same city are importing from abroad, each side may have an abundance of private information.

Second, a number of factors conspire to impede access to information about trader efforts. Many transactions involve several middlemen. If punishment should only occur if a certain behavior was intentional, the presence of many middlemen can make it hard to assess culpability. Language barriers with foreign suppliers can also make it hard to know whether receiving a product different from what was ordered was a mistake or intentional.

Third, in complicated operating environments, it may be hard for two parties to determine what actions constitute a breach of an agreement. Clarity on

9 See Appendix Table C.1.

what is defection, which is critical for relational contracting, emerges over time (2012, p. 8).

Fourth, there are hurdles to generating a public reputation. When relational contracting is conceptualized as being sustained due to fears of damaging one's public reputation, two additional conditions must be satisfied. First, others must know when an individual is cheated. Many studies unrealistically assume that communication among traders is costless (e.g., Klein and Leffler, 1981). However, this is not always the case: when traders directly compete with each other, they have few incentives to tell others if they have been cheated. In fact, they may even want their competitors to be cheated.

Data from Lagos suggest that there are substantial hurdles to creating a functioning reputational mechanism. Traders report that they rarely reveal the identity of their main supplier to other traders. Were a trader to introduce a fellow trader to a supplier, typically a contract between the two traders would be written to specify that the trader doing the introducing will receive a cut of the profits from the second trader's first purchase from the new supplier. Given that supplier identity alone is so secretive, it seems unlikely that information about specific dubious suppliers would easily spread.

In short, a specific set of conditions must be met for relational contracting to operate, and these conditions are frequently absent in places like urban Nigeria. It is much more common to find long-term trading relationships supplemented by resource-intensive monitoring to encourage honest behavior. For example, Meredith Startz (2018) shows that 32 percent of Nigerian importers in her study personally traveled to the source country, often China, to inspect the goods themselves. The costliness of this strategy suggests the severity of the contracting problems. Startz finds that traders continue to travel for purchases from even long-term suppliers. This highlights the importance of third-party contract enforcement, be it private or public.

4.7 ALTERNATIVE EXPLANATIONS

The design of this project allows me to control for a variety of factors that could affect private governance, such as a country's regime. But my argument could coexist with other explanations of variation in private governance. In this section I assess the theoretical plausibility of additional explanations of private good governance. First, I consider explanations about factors that might shape traders' ability to act collectively to constrain predatory leader behavior. Second, I investigate whether private good governance may be more critical for certain *types* of products, which may drive the provision of private pro-trade policies. Last, I consider whether individual sorting into well-governed groups could explain the outcome. In Chapters 5 and 6 I assess these and other explanations empirically.

What prevents group members from overthrowing or sanctioning a predatory leader? There are three ways that group members can pressure their leaders to refrain from extorting. First, the logic of group monitoring of public officials may apply to group member monitoring of group leaders. When a leaders is "structurally embedded" in the community they serve, their desire for social acceptance in other spheres of their life can motivate good governance (Granovetter, 1985; Tsai, 2007; Uzzi, 1996). In many urban contexts, though, such embeddedness is rare. Group leaders may be "culturally embedded" (Post, 2014), but they are rarely as structurally embedded as might happen in more rural settings. A second possibility is for group members to partner with third parties to sanction their leaders.[10] This would require a group to overcome the collective action problem in the absence of their leader, which is no easy feat. Third, there are compelling arguments about how group cooperation is facilitated by sanctioning those who act opportunistically (e.g., Miguel and Gugerty, 2005). While this literature lacks substantive accounts of such sanctioning, leaving unanswered important questions about how and when it occurs, a leader is almost certainly required to initiate these decisions. It is unclear what mechanism a group would use to sanction its leaders; I expect this to be unusual in practice.

If sanctioning is difficult, the obstacles to mutiny are enormous (Leeson, 2007). Mutiny is, first and foremost, a collective action problem. Such problems are normally overcome under the guidance of a leader, but in cases of potential mutiny, the recognized leader is, by definition, not involved in the process. Normally a new leader must be identified, which, as noted earlier, is not straightforward. Further, mutiny is exceptionally risky. Group members must trust that a large number of their fellow group members will follow through on a promise to revolt. But paradoxically, in groups where mutiny is desirable, a predatory group leader has probably cultivated distrust among group members. Finally, in many – though not all – groups, the group leader has state recognition. This can make mutiny even more difficult, depending on the extent of such recognition. In short, while group sanctioning of a leader and mutiny are theoretically possible, they are likely to be empirically rare.

With these hurdles in mind, I consider factors that might enable sanctioning. Variation in group member social embeddedness shapes members' ability to constrain leader behavior. If group members live in the same community, or attend the same churches or mosques, they may be better able to overcome the collective action problem inherent in challenging leadership.

Group size could also matter. Mancur Olson, for instance, has suggested that smaller associations should be better able to cooperate (1965). Smaller groups might also be more successful at challenging group leaders.

Group leaders who share the ethnicity of group members may feel more affinity toward them and be less likely to predate. There is evidence, however, that group leaders can capitalize on group homogeneity to facilitate extortion and consolidate power (Acemoglu, Reed and Robinson, 2014; Berman, 1997).[11] I expect that group homogeneity will not be sufficient for private pro-trade policies.

---

[10] This would be analogous to the logic in Markus (2012).

[11] See also Mattingly (2016) for a discussion of how the state can use local elites to expropriate from their informal constituents.

Yet group homogeneity could support private good governance in other ways. Studies have shown that shared ethnicity can create trust and promote cooperation (Habyarimana, 2009) and enable economic growth (Easterly and Levine, 1997; Robinson, 2016). Perhaps this could make it easier for leaders to elicit sensitive information about suppliers and customers. However, members of trade unions and business associations are often in competition with each other. Therefore, even in small groups, shared ethnicity may not be sufficient to overcome competitive forces.

A related possibility is that private governance is less important for homogenous groups. Members of these groups may share information about dubious trading partners organically, and private governance may be poor simply because trader cooperation obviates the need for it. However, unstructured cooperation is unusual for large groups; it typically requires leaders.

An additional alternative explanation is that the types of products sold in a market could potentially shape private governance. For instance, information sharing about dubious suppliers may be less important when the quality of a product can be easily observed upon inspection (e.g., a plate versus a bottle of wine). However, this should not alter the incentives for private extortion, and empirically, there are opportunities for sellers of all products to cheat buyers.

My argument rests on the assumption that group members aim to maximize their income, which depends in part on whether they are part of a group that has pro-trade policies. A potential criticism of the argument is that successful traders select into trade-promoting groups and are more likely to be better market leaders, and that this may explain the persistence of private pro-trade institutions rather than the mutual threat argument. I expect, however, that there will be substantial frictions associated with sorting into trade-promoting groups, because (1) group membership is relatively sticky, making it difficult for individuals to frequently switch groups and (2) outsiders have highly incomplete information about the conditions in the group before joining. These assumptions may not hold for all groups everywhere, but I expect they will hold for many groups. For example, American prison gangs are often organized by race. This can make switching gangs difficult, as there may be only one gang that would welcome an individual as a member (Skarbek, 2014, pp. 112–113).

4.8 CONCLUSION

In this chapter I discussed three local public goods that group leaders can offer: (1) impartial dispute resolution, (2) information sharing, and (3) proper accounting for private fee collection. Given the hurdles to providing these services – for example, individuals wanting to keep valuable information to themselves – these services are less likely to emerge in the absence of a group leader. And even with a group leader, these services will not always be provided. When government officials threaten to interfere in the group, under certain conditions, group leaders will provide these services – not necessarily for benevolent purposes, but rather to be able to organize group members to fend off these threats and to reduce the likelihood that disputes will tempt government officials to intervene. When group members are competing with each other, the hurdles to these services are greater, and groups may get stuck in an equilibrium that does not support trade.

Simply because a group leader acquired the position through popular election – as many leaders do – does not imply that the leader will have the support necessary to threaten politicians. Meaningful threats against politicians require support that is deep (because credible threats must be costly to group members) and broad (because threats will be more effective when a protest, for example, includes all group members). Winning a plurality of votes will not guarantee this level of support.

I showed that relational contracting is not ubiquitous, and thus groups with and without trade-promoting institutions cannot solve contracting problems with long-term relationships alone. I also discussed the limits to alternative paths to good private governance. Group members often lack the ability to motivate their leader to improve their business environment. Further, the logistics of switching groups can leave individuals in unsupportive environments for longer than they desire and result in unprofitable groups persisting longer than seems possible. In the next chapter, I test these predictions with in-depth investigations of four markets.

My argument may extend to accounts of private policing in nineteenth-century California, where private police forces emerged in *response* to predatory public police (Stringham, 2015). The argument may also apply to claim clubs, informal governments of squatters on frontier land in the nineteenth-century American West. These informal governments operated in the face of severe government threats to sell this publicly owned land (Murtazashvili, 2013). My argument could also shed light on informal transport associations. For instance, in Jamaica, there is evidence of minibus association member communication "[t]o reduce the incursion of the police on their activities" (Cervero and Golub, 2011, p. 508).

I leave unanswered questions about when and how market leader governance could change for future research, in part because the data in Chapter 6 relate to a single point in time, and it proved difficult to acquire historical information about the specific policies of previous market leaders in the case studies in Chapter 5. However, in his study of American prison gangs, Skarbek offers some intriguing possibilities (2014). Prior to the 1970s, there was a convict code about proper prisoner behavior – for example, never rat on an inmate. As the population of American prisons grew, and as the prison population became younger, respect for the code weakened, which increased the demand for gangs. In more general terms, diversifying group membership weakened norms and made more formal rules more important.

While I do not think the need for protection organizations will always lead to their creation, it may make their emergence more likely. A related question is whether constant threats are necessary to keep group leaders in check, or whether a single threat could push them to implement pro-trade policies. Testing how these types of exogenous trends (or shocks) change the nature of private governance is an exciting area for future work.

5

Government Threats and Group Leader Strength

Market association dynamics can be something of a black box, even to customers who frequent them. In this chapter I look at four markets, demystifying leadership behavior and the role of politics, and testing the part of my theory that focuses on threats and leader strength. The first market, Oke Arin, is an archetype of private good governance, with a market leader who maintains sophisticated pro-trade policies. I assess the extent to which the conditions that sustain these policies are consistent with my theory about leaders.

The other three markets, Ebe Ebe, Dabiri, and Destiny,[1] are governed by leaders who do not implement trade-promoting policies. These markets are therefore not supportive environments in which to be a trader. Prior studies assume that such groups disappear quickly, as current group members abandon them and prospective group members decide not to join. I document that these groups can persist for much longer than previously assumed.

The case of Ebe Ebe highlights a special type of group: one in which the group leader extorts from his or her own members. Previous studies have assumed that group members are mobile and would simply move to a better group if a leader attempted to extort from them, and that group leaders would therefore refrain from extorting for fear of losing members. But this cannot be taken for granted. The Ebe Ebe market illustrates how predatory leaders exploit traders' immobility. Additionally, research often implies that a strong leader with the *ability* to create and enforce formal private governance rules is sufficient for pro-trade policies. Ebe Ebe provides an account of the perils of having a strong leader who is not motivated to use his power to promote trade. This phenomenon has been widely documented in research on public governance – we know that strong, authoritarian governments can have pernicious effects on citizen welfare – but these cases have been ignored in research

---

[1] I have changed the names of these markets to protect the identity of respondents who shared sensitive information. I have not changed the name of Oke Arin, on request of the trader who served as the most valuable informant on this case. Additionally, I cannot think of any way in which information from Oke Arin would be embarrassing or get any individual in trouble.

on private governance. This study is among the first to examine the potential negative effects of strong leadership on private governance.

Dabiri is a different type of badly governed market. It has a well-intentioned but weak leader who does not extort from her group, and from the traders like her. However, she does not promote trade and has not been able to resist government encroachment which could destroy the market.

The Destiny market has weak leadership that, for idiosyncratic reasons related to the presence of a larger umbrella association, does not face government threats. The market leadership has paralyzing divisions and does not provide trade-promoting services.

To determine what else might explain variation across these markets, I explore two potential explanatory variables: (1) whether ethnically homogeneous markets select better leaders and (2) whether market leaders who have long time horizons (leaders who plan to serve as the leader for the long term) govern better because they want the market to grow. I systematically assess the explanatory value of these variables using data from the four markets, and show that they cannot explain the outcome. I conclude by explaining why, despite being inhospitable to trade, the three badly governed markets remain open.

I use within-case analysis methods to make inferences about the conditions that enable or impede market leader good governance (Brady and Collier, 2010; Goertz and Mahoney, 2012). I identify the processes that sustain the current stable arrangements in these markets and assess the extent to which they are consistent with my argument.

The Oke Arin, Dabiri, and Destiny markets were chosen by randomly selecting markets from the survey data on the explanatory variables.[2] I chose Ebe Ebe since it was a market with predatory leaders where traders were willing to speak with me. Table 5.1 shows the distribution of these markets across the explanatory variables.

TABLE 5.1 *Distribution of market case studies across explanatory variables.*

	Government threats	No government threats
Strong leader	Oke Arin	Ebe Ebe
Weak leader	Dabiri	Destiny

---

[2] An earlier version of this project conceptualized government threats solely based on whether markets were located in jurisdictions with interventionist local governments. The cases were selected using this conceptualization. I subsetted the survey data to markets with strong and weak leaders in interventionist and noninterventionist local governments and randomly selected markets from each of these categories. Destiny was one of these markets. In the first markets selected in the strong-threat and weak-threat categories, I was not able to get traders or market executives to speak with me openly. I randomly selected new markets in each of these categories, and those markets were Oke Arin and Dabiri.

I personally conducted interviews in all of these markets. I hired research assistants to conduct additional interviews to obtain the perspective of more traders.

5.1 A MARKET WHERE CITIZENS ARREST NORM VIOLATORS: THE CASE OF OKE ARIN

Oke Arin is a strong market that faces government threats. I expect it to have trade-promoting policies, and that is what I observe. Why is this market a paragon of good private governance? Much of the evidence from this market is broadly consistent with the theory that external government threats motivate the private provision of order. Specifically, the leader (1) implements pro-trade policies to limit state interference – in this case from the National Agency for Food and Drug Administration and Control (NAFDAC) and (2) avoids extorting from traders so as to be able to mobilize them to fend off threats from extractive local politicians.

5.1.1 Trade-Promoting Policies

Oke Arin is spread throughout a series of narrow and crowded streets on Lagos Island. Traders sell mostly wine, but also meat, baking items, and nonalcoholic beverages. The market occupies the western corner of Lagos Island which has been registered as a market area for decades. In 2004 many Igbo traders on the Island pooled funds to lease land for a new and larger market on the outskirts of the city. As thousands of traders set up shops in this new market, existing organizations on Lagos Island, including the Balogun Business Association, were dismantled. The Oke Arin market association emerged in the city center during this process.

The market has a president and executive committee, all of whom are elected to four-year terms. Ten line leaders head smaller units of the market.

Market leaders will lose their position if they fail to properly account for the fees they collect from traders.[3] For example, at one market meeting, a line treasurer was asked to detail how his fees were accounted for. Traders and more senior market leaders realized the numbers did not add up. People at the meeting "were not happy because they felt duped out of their fees," one trader said. "The account statement was clear to all of us."[4] The treasurer lost his position immediately. "Everybody in the market knew about it and was in support," the trader said.

Oke Arin has private policies that unequivocally promote trade. In monthly meetings the market leader shares information about dubious suppliers and companies to avoid doing business with. This helps traders directly, since they will be less likely to buy products they cannot sell. It also helps them indirectly:

---

[3] In the survey data, both of the Oke Arin traders reported that the market leaders properly account for the fees they collected.

[4] Interview with trader I on August 7, 2017.

when their fellow traders sell safe products, customers will be more likely to shop in the market without fear of being duped.

In many markets, traders avoid reporting on suppliers who cheated them because they are in competition with other traders in the market. They might, in fact, *want* their neighbors to be cheated by a supplier they were cheated by. In Oke Arin, however, traders are motivated to report opportunistic behavior. This is not because traders have high levels of social capital, but rather because the market leader will help to resolve the *immediate* dispute. When alerted to opportunistic suppliers, Oke Arin leaders will punish them, and in some cases apprehend these individuals through "citizen's arrests" and ban them from doing business in the market. This private benefit motivates members to contribute to a club good, essentially a directory of individuals to avoid.

All traders interviewed confirmed that information sharing about dubious customers and suppliers takes place.[5] "The executives have warned us about 419 customers," one trader said, using the local term for those who cheat others.[6] When leaders share this information, "we are able to ensure we don't get tricked," another trader said.[7] The result of this information is that "every trader becomes careful of taking any supplier that would spoil their market."[8]

There is aggressive in-group policing in Oke Arin: the market leader punishes traders who break the rules or sell substandard goods in order to maintain the market's reputation of supplying quality products. The leader confiscates any substandard products traders are selling. If the trader had been knowingly buying from a supplier who was banned from the market, the market leader might lock the shop to prevent trading. According to one trader, market leaders tell traders that "whatever happens to any trader that does her own thing" – that is, does not abide by market rules – "she is on her own." The trader noted that there are still always a few traders who do their own thing. When NAFDAC officials came to the market, the market leaders directed them to these traders.[9] The in-group policing strategy relies in part on customers. If customers purchase substandard products, they report the trader to the market executives.[10]

When handling disputes between traders and suppliers, or traders and customers, the market leaders do not necessarily side with the traders. One trader recalled a time when a trader failed to pay his supplier. The leaders came to mediate and ultimately forced the trader to pay the supplier within one month.[11] "The leaders are very truthful," another trader added. "They don't

---

5 Interviews with traders E and F on August 1, 2017, and traders G, H, and I on August 3, 2017. In the survey, one of the two Oke Arin traders said the market leaders share information about dubious customers and suppliers.
6 Interview with trader E on August 1, 2017.
7 Interview with trader H on August 3, 2017.
8 Interview with trader I on August 3, 2017.
9 Interview with trader I on August 7, 2017.
10 Interview with market executive B on January 19, 2016.
11 Interview with trader F on August 1, 2017.

favor anyone."[12] He recalled a time when a customer complained to the executives after being sold a fake drink without a NAFDAC number. The market leaders assessed the situation and told the trader to give the customer a replacement.

Of course, if a supplier or customer is in the wrong, the leaders will punish these individuals. Yet adjudicating guilt is not simple. A customer may untruthfully claim they have been cheated in order to obtain a refund. The market leaders invest time to determine who is at fault. If a customer says a trader is selling substandard products, a line leader might secretly keep an eye on the trader's shop for a few days to figure out if this is true.[13]

Market conditions in Oke Arin reflect the market leaders' policies. Security is not a problem in the market,[14] since the leaders employ private security guards who work "round the clock."[15] The market executives work with two government agencies, the Central Business District and the Kick Against Indiscipline, to keep street vendors away from the market.[16] Street vendors – who sell illegally from blankets or small wooden tables on the sidewalk or street – may sell the same product as market traders and can thus take business away from traders with shops.

When asked whether the market leaders help his business in any way, one trader explained the connection between leader governance and sales: "The way we are asked to sell only correct goods, it helps me and my neighbors not to trick people. This has helped us to do the right things and get the correct money."[17]

5.1.2 Why Is This Market Governed So Well?

Oke Arin market leaders maintain trade-promoting policies like information sharing and in-group policing because they are strong and face consistent threats of government intrusion.

There is substantial evidence that the market leadership is strong. The leaders have regularly scheduled meetings on the last Thursday of every month at 3 pm in a nearby church. Everyone is expected to attend; all shops in the market are expected to be locked, and there is always a large turnout.[18] "People see this," the market leader said, referencing the visually striking occurrence of all shops being locked. "Everyone knows we are strong."[19] Consistent with

---

[12] Interview with trader H on August 3, 2017.
[13] Interview with market executive B on January 19, 2016.
[14] Interviews with traders G and H on August 3, 2017.
[15] Interview with trader G on August 3, 2017.
[16] Interview with trader G on August 3, 2017.
[17] Interview with trader H on August 3, 2017.
[18] Interviews with traders E and F on August 1, 2017, and traders G and H on August 3, 2017. The two Oke Arin traders surveyed also reported that there were regularly scheduled meetings for traders.
[19] Interview with market executive B on April 21, 2015.

the theoretical expectation that the level of market leader strength is persistent, these market meetings have been taking place since at least 1997.[20]

The market leaders are independently strong; there does not appear to be any collusion with the local government. "The local government does not put mouth in our meetings," one trader said, using a phrase to reference interference.[21]

For years, Oke Arin has faced two types of persistent government threats, each of which clearly illustrates one of the two mechanisms through which threats motivate private good governance. Local government threats coexist with an absence of private extortion, which allows market leaders to mobilize traders in order to fend off these threats. And the threat of NAFDAC interference motivates impartial dispute resolution.

The first threat comes from the local government, which has been continuously interventionist. If government threats are largely a function of a market's profitability, this would challenge the argument that these threats motivate good market governance. But that does not appear to be the case. Since its formation, the Lagos Island West local government has been aggressively trying to raise tax revenue from the market.

The persistence of local government interference can be attributed to characteristics that are uncorrelated with the market's success. Many traditional, wealthy families have their palaces in Lagos Island West, and it is accepted that local government chairmen will come from one of these families. The first local government chairperson was Aderinola Disu, from the Akinsemoyin Royal Family, which owned substantial land. In the early 2000s the economic interests of the traditional families in Lagos Island were under threat, as decaying infrastructure and the presence of thugs pushed many businesses off the Island. In response, the land owners formed a coalition, and Disu – a prominent member of this coalition – successfully sought the nomination of the Alliance for Democracy Party, the precursor to the All Progressives Congress (APC).[22] Disu's emergence was tied to the economic *problems* plaguing the area during the time of her election.[23]

My earlier assertion that politicians with higher public sector career ambitions will be more likely to intervene in organized societal groups in their jurisdiction is consistent with Disu's behavior and career trajectory. Since being appointed to the boards of two state agencies "[a]s a reward for exemplary performance as the Chairman of the Lagos Island Local Government," she has worked as the Special Advisor on the Central Business Districts, a high state government-level position.

[20] Interview with trader E on August 1, 2017.
[21] Interview with trader H on August 3, 2017.
[22] Interview by email with former politician A on June 24, 2015.
[23] While Disu's engagement in the community during her tenure is undoubtedly tied to the area's business potential, it does *not* seem to be the case that strong, successful market leaders pressured the ruling party to nominate a certain *type* of politician.

In 2006 Disu tried to increase taxes in Oke Arin, but the market leaders claimed that a local official had promised that its traders would never have to pay more than N5,500/year ($15) in fees to the local government. In 2006 the market took the local government to court. The case was not resolved until a year into the tenure of the subsequent chairman, Eshinlokun Sanni Wasiu Olatunji,[24] when the judge ordered the parties to settle out of court. The market and local government agreed on N6,500/shop/year ($18), which was N2,000 less than the government's request for 2006. That Olatunji continued to pursue the case underscores the persistence of local government interventionism, while Oke Arin's legal challenge is indicative of the market leader's willingness to fight back.

When asked what threats the market could make against the local government at the time and how the government could pressure the market leaders, a former politician said:

The powers the markets had over the local government were first, in a Democratic Dispensation there is freedom of expression and exercise of fundamental human rights by seeking relief through legal channels. [...] Conversely the powers the local government had over the traders were legal and entrenched in the 1999 Constitution of The Federal Republic Of Nigeria, Schedule IV [a reference to the right to tax markets].[25]

The court case with the local government is evidence of the market leader's commitment to managing public taxation, and in the survey, no trader in Oke Arin reported that local government officials ever show up unannounced to collect fees. As noted earlier, almost all traders reported that the market leader did not extort from them. This makes sense, since the leader needs to mobilize the traders' support to keep the lawsuit going.

The second threat comes from NAFDAC. Because the Oke Arin market sells food and beverages, its traders have frequent interactions with the agency,[26] which has the authority to punish those who sell falsely branded products by confiscating goods,[27] locking shops, imposing fines, or even arresting traders.[28] When NAFDAC officials intervene in the market, they are accompanied by the Mobile Police, who come in pick-up trucks, with guns pointed out the windows. This is a rent-seeking opportunity, which scares customers away.

Traders perceive NAFDAC as a salient threat. "NAFDAC people are disturbing us," one trader said. They enter the market and demand to see

---

[24] Consistent with my argument, Olatunji also had higher career ambitions, and in 2015, he became a member of the Lagos State House of Assembly.

[25] Interview by email with former politician A on June 23, 2015.

[26] See, for example, Abimbola Akosile, "NAFDAC Docks Four Over Counterfeit Products," *This Day*, October 26, 2014, thisdaylive.com/articles/nafdac-docks-four-over-counterfeit-products/192266/ (accessed May 30, 2015); Kenechukwu Ezeonyejiaku, "NAF-DAC Uncovers Illegal Production Facilities, Counterfeiters," *The Guardian*, October 23, 2014, allafrica.com/stories/201410231259.html (accessed May 30, 2015).

[27] Interview with trader H on August 3, 2017.

[28] Interview with trader G on August 3, 2017.

products' NAFDAC numbers. "They are almost entering on and off every two weeks and lock some stalls together with the police."[29] "The police are always here," another trader said.[30]

This direct evidence is consistent with the mechanism of implementing in-group policing and information sharing to keep the government out of market affairs. In this case, the market leader conducts in-group policing by punishing his own traders for cheating others, and shares information about fraudsters to reduce the likelihood of NAFDAC carrying out more raids.[31] Indeed, the market leader himself said that he polices the traders' behavior to reduce the likelihood of NAFDAC intervention.[32] The market leaders seem to have the long-term interests of the traders at heart. One trader noted that, following a NAFDAC raid, "some of the affected people were upset that the market executive did not give them prior notice."[33] "The market leaders have warned us not to sell fake goods," another trader noted.[34]

Although a small number of traders sell wine and beverages in the Dabiri market, which is discussed in more detail later, NAFDAC pays no attention to that market. This is most likely because many more traders in Oke Arin sell wine.

According to my theory, when market leaders do not extort from their group members, they can mobilize their traders to fend off government threats. When market leaders are capable of mobilizing traders in this way, politicians will be more likely to desire the leader's political support.

This is what happens in Oke Arin. Multiple traders report that politicians campaigned in the market preceding the July 2017 local government elections, meeting with both traders and market leaders.[35] A market leader I interviewed showed me a poster given to him by people campaigning for the then president Goodluck Jonathan during the 2015 general elections. One trader reported that, when politicians come, they often bring money, sing songs, and make promises related to the market.[36]

The market line leaders mobilize the traders on their line during the campaigning.[37] One trader reported that the leaders asked the traders to come and see the politicians as they campaigned in the summer of 2017.[38] While many of the traders in this market are Igbo, who are traditionally thought to support the Peoples Democratic Party, one trader noted that "we have to support APC despite the variance in political affiliations here," though not all traders agreed

[29] Interview with trader F on August 1, 2017.
[30] Interview with trader H on August 3, 2017.
[31] Interview with trader I on August 7, 2017.
[32] Interview with market executive B on April 21, 2015.
[33] Interview with trader G on August 3, 2017.
[34] Interview with trader H on August 3, 2017.
[35] Interviews with traders E and F on August 1, 2017, and traders G, H, and I on August 3, 2017.
[36] Interview with trader F on August 1, 2017.
[37] Interview with trader I on August 7, 2017.
[38] Interview with trader H on August 3, 2017.

with the assessment that market leaders pressured group members to support the APC.

The market leaders mobilize traders in non-election periods as well. One trader recalled that they were encouraged to attend a meeting with NAFDAC officials, which led to NAFDAC unsealing some shops they had locked and a more friendly relationship with the agency.[39]

For the market leader to keep the local government in check, the leader's threats to mobilize traders to support or protest against certain candidates must be credible. How can we be sure politicians perceive the market executives as strong and their threats as credible? Representatives of both the leading presidential contenders visited the Oke Arin market association in 2015 to solicit their support. Gubernatorial and senatorial candidates came as well. As the theory predicts, the Oke Arin market leader endorses political candidates. He also conducts question-and-answer sessions with traders at the monthly meetings in front of politicians to demonstrate his ability to influence traders' positions.[40]

5.2 "I DON'T KNOW WHAT THEY ARE USING THE MONEY FOR": THE CASE OF EBE EBE

Ebe Ebe is a strong market that does not face state threats. It is predicted to have a leader who extorts, and that is what I observed. Ebe Ebe was formed around 1988.[41] The Lagos state government had just demolished a large slum and the residents relocated a few miles away, creating Ebe Ebe in their new community. In 2014 the market was demolished and renovated, and officially reopened in 2016. Though the current market leaders are the same as before, most of the traders who had shops before the renovation were priced out of the new "ultramodern" market. Today, shops go for N550,000 to N14,000,000 ($1,528–$38,889), depending on their size.[42]

Because many of the traders are new, they feel that the market leadership was imposed on them.[43] The market leader is about seventy-five years old and holds his position for life.[44]

Most traders interviewed felt that the market leaders were not accounting properly for the fees they collect.[45] Trader A noted that market leaders say the market dues are used to pay for ten security guards, but there are only four. Leaders say each security guard is paid N30,000 ($83) per month, but in fact

---

[39] Interview with trader G on August 3, 2017.

[40] While scholars have documented that politicians can assess brokers based on their ability to mobilize voters (e.g., Szwarcberg, 2015), observing brokers' powers of persuasion firsthand could be another assessment strategy.

[41] To protect the anonymity of respondents and this market, this is not the precise date.

[42] Interview with market manager A on August 5, 2017.

[43] Interview with trader C on August 1, 2017.

[44] Interview with market executive A on August 4, 2017.

[45] In the survey, three of the seven Ebe Ebe traders said the market leaders do not properly account for fees.

the guards are paid N20,000 ($56) per month. This same trader believes that the ban on personal electricity meters is another opportunity for market leaders to seek rents. The leaders have an arrangement with the power company in which they pay less than what they collect from traders for electricity.[46]

Trader A is not the only one who believes the market leaders are not accounting properly for the fees they collect. "It is obvious they don't settle the people who are supposed to carry out dirt in this market," another trader said, referencing the fact that traders are paying for waste collection, but the trash is not collected frequently.[47] There are heaps of waste, according to trader A. "I don't know what they are using the money for. I don't know."[48] Another trader said he has not seen anything to convince him that the leaders are accounting properly for fees.[49]

All traders interviewed said the market leaders never shared information about dubious customers or suppliers.[50] Similarly, in the survey, only one of eight traders said the market leaders shared information about customers and suppliers. Traders also reported that the leaders do not help resolve market disputes; disputes are expected to be resolved by the trader and customer or by the trader and supplier.[51]

A number of infrastructural deficiencies further inhibit trade. For example, the leaders do not prevent hawkers from selling near the market and disrupting market trade.[52] Though security is not a serious concern in this market, a security guard was caught stealing just prior to these interviews.[53] It is possible that this theft was related to the guards being underpaid. In addition, though the market renovation was supposed to solve problems related to drainage, it did not: in July 2017 the market flooded and was inaccessible for two days.[54]

Because the market leaders charge such high rents for the shops, traders are forced to charge high prices which drive customers away according to one trader.[55] Moreover, the market leaders charge N100 ($0.28) for parking, which traders believe deters customers. "You can imagine if you send your driver to buy a good that is N500 ($1.39), and that is the only money on him, when he wants to enter the market, they will collect N100 ($0.28) and he will be left with N400 ($1.11), which means he will not be able to buy what he wants. That is the problem we are facing."[56]

[46] Interview with trader A on August 1, 2017.
[47] Interview with trader B on August 1, 2017.
[48] Interview with trader A on August 1, 2017.
[49] Interview with trader C on August 1, 2017.
[50] Interviews with traders A, B, C, and D on August 1, 2017.
[51] Interview with trader A on August 1, 2017.
[52] Interview with trader A on August 1, 2017.
[53] Interview with trader A on August 1, 2017.
[54] Interview with trader D on August 1, 2017.
[55] Interview with trader D on August 1, 2017.
[56] Interview with trader A on August 1, 2017.

5.2.1   What Explains Private Extortion?

The market executives in Ebe Ebe are strong, in the sense that they can control market affairs. Seven of the eight surveyed traders said the market leaders hold scheduled meetings regularly for traders, which either the trader or a representative (like a salesboy or salesgirl) is required to attend.[57]

The market has few problems with the government. The local government asks for a variety of high fees, but the traders have successfully negotiated these fees down on an individual basis.[58] The police and NAFDAC have not entered the market recently.[59] Two traders said the police are not allowed to enter the market,[60] a situation that is not uncommon in markets with strong leaders. Traders are not permitted to call the police if there is a dispute between two traders: the market leader must resolve the issue. "The leadership doesn't give room for any penetration by the police," one trader said, adding that this is "strongly spelled out in the constitution of the market association."[61] A wine trader – the type of trader who would be most likely to interact with NAFDAC officials – said there have been no signs of NAFDAC presence in the market.[62]

According to my theory, in the absence of government threats, the market leader will not need to mobilize traders to push back against the government. And when traders are not voting as a bloc, politicians will be less likely to campaign in the market. Consistent with this hypothesis, traders in Ebe Ebe report no campaigning inside the market. When interviews were conducted in this market, local government elections were expected to be held shortly. Traders reported that politicians, by coincidence, had a meeting place in the Ebe Ebe area, but they never visited traders to influence their vote.[63] "The politicians do meet by the parking lot, but they don't disturb us," one trader said.[64] One trader reported that, during the 2015 general elections, "some political parties came to mobilize the people, but the turnout was very poor."[65]

5.3   "THEY ARE NONCHALANT": THE CASE OF UNENGAGED MARKET LEADERS IN DABIRI

Like Ebe Ebe, the Dabiri market lacks pro-trade policies, but, unlike Ebe Ebe, the Dabiri market leader does *not* extort from her members. The Dabiri market shows that public extortion will plague markets that face state threats and lack strong leaders to defend themselves. This section explores why a well-liked,

---

[57] Interviews with traders A, C, and D on August 1, 2017.

[58] Interview with trader A on August 1, 2017.

[59] Interviews with traders A, B, and C on August 1, 2017.

[60] Interviews with market executive A on August 4, 2017, and trader C on August 1, 2017.

[61] Interview with market executive A on August 4, 2017.

[62] Interview with trader D on August 1, 2017.

[63] Interview with trader A on August 1, 2017.

[64] Interview with trader B on August 1, 2017.

[65] Interview with trader C on August 1, 2017.

well-intentioned market leader is not sufficient for the provision of private trade-promoting policies.

Dabiri's market leader was elected via free and fair elections and is well liked by the traders. The traders value her education – she has a master's degree in secretarial studies from the United Kingdom, which is often perceived as an important characteristic in a market leader, as they must negotiate with government officials.[66]

The market is located off a busy expressway on local government land, but, like many markets, its management has been handed over to a private managing director, who was given a lease on the market. This man serves as the market owner, and he has two managers who oversee tasks such as rent collection.[67]

5.3.1 Absence of Trade-Promoting Policies

Most traders feel that the market leader accounts properly for the fees she collects.[68] "Every fee has a reason," one trader said.[69]

Yet public extortion is a problem: in 2014 the local government increased taxes by 100 percent "by force," according to a market manager.[70] The traders pay a confusing plethora of fees that they often do not understand sufficiently to explain to an outsider. Moreover, the market leader takes a hands-off approach to market management: while she does not extort from traders, she does not enact policies that could support contractual trade. Traders say they never call on her to resolve disputes with suppliers.

In the interviews and surveys, the traders all reported that the market leader does not share information about customers or suppliers.[71] "It is a personal issue," one trader said.[72] The market leader is "nonchalant," one trader said,[73] expressing a common sentiment among traders. There are no regularly scheduled meetings in the market, only emergency meetings,[74] which only 20 percent of the traders attend.[75]

Impartial dispute resolution is easier said than done. If a market leader impartially mediates disagreements between traders and outside trading partners, outsiders will feel more comfortable doing business in the market. But

---

[66] Looking at slum leaders in India, Auerbach and Thachil (2018) find that slum residents value education as a proxy for efficacy when selecting leaders. The case of Dabiri suggests similar patterns might be present in Lagos.

[67] Interview with market manager B on August 3, 2017.

[68] Interview with traders J, K, and L on July 31, 2017. In the survey data, the one Dabiri trader who responded to this question said the market leader did not properly account for fees.

[69] Interview with trader K on July 13, 2017.

[70] Interview with market manager C on September 26, 2014.

[71] Interviews with traders J and L on July 31, 2017, and trader M on August 1, 2017.

[72] Interview with trader M on August 1, 2017.

[73] Interview with trader L on July 31, 2017.

[74] Interviews with traders J, K, and L on July 31, 2017. In the survey, two of the four surveyed traders said there were regular meetings for traders.

[75] Interview with trader J on July 31, 2017.

from the perspective of the market leader, fair dispute resolution is both time-consuming and taxing on social capital. Since the guilty party is unlikely to admit to being at fault, the leader will have to spend time investigating the circumstances. Additionally, ruling against a market trader who the leader sees every day requires determination and a long-term view of the market's success.

Consistent with my theory, the Dabiri market leader does not impartially mediate disputes. Some traders felt the market leader did not intervene in disputes at all, while others felt that she tended to side with the traders: "they will intervene and definitely take sides with us here," one trader said.[76] "Of course they will side with the trader, but we no dey fight here o," another trader said.[77]

Though sales in the market improved slightly in early 2017, they were generally perceived to be bad. Three traders reported that the lack of customers was the main issue facing the market.[78] One trader, who sells a variety of items including toiletries, staples, drinks, textbooks, and electronics, said she used to sell canned goods and baking items. But because of low sales, she was frequently forced to throw away expired goods. She decided to diversify and sell fewer goods that could expire.[79]

There are a number of possible explanations for the market's low sales. One is the illegal presence of street vendors on the main road outside the market.[80] These vendors sell the same products as the market traders, at lower prices, which tempts customers to shop there instead of parking and entering the market. The market's inadequate drainage system further motivates customers to buy from street vendors. Even after a light rain, walking around the market involves being shin-deep in water. Every time I visited the market, the traders I interviewed during my previous visit had gone out of business in part due to the street vendors.

Other challenges result from the absence of trade-promoting policies such as sharing information about dubious suppliers, because of which traders get cheated by suppliers. For example, one trader has a supplier with whom he has been trading for five years who still hides expired goods at the bottom of a carton of products.[81]

5.3.2 Explaining the Absence of Trade-Promoting Policies

The Dabiri market association has been weak since its inception, in part due to divisions in the market. In the early 2000s a local traditional leader, or king, gave the market's land to the local government. When the market was built, the king was given allocation papers for several of the shops to distribute as he

---

[76] Interview with trader K on July 31, 2017.
[77] Interview with trader L on July 31, 2017.
[78] Interviews with traders K, L, and M on July 31, 2017.
[79] Interview with trader J on July 31, 2017.
[80] Interview with trader M on August 1, 2017.
[81] Interview with trader K on July 31, 2017.

wished. Similarly, the former local government chairman was given allocation papers, which he gave to supporters and members of his family. The remaining shops' leases were sold competitively. Many of the primary leaseholders leased their shops to other people, because they were either living abroad or too busy to manage a shop, but some traders are the primary leaseholders. This diversity of ownership status among the active traders in the market has caused frequent disputes over how to respond to increases in local government taxes and fees. Secondary leaseholders might not be opposed to a fee that would affect the primary leaseholders, and vice versa. When there is uncertainty over whether a fee would affect primary or secondary leaseholders, there are further disputes.

These divisions are not the only impediment to the market leader's ability to control affairs in the market. The leader has other businesses outside the market, including a restaurant, which distracts her from market affairs. She is further weakened by the presence of the market managers.[82]

The market leader is also weakened by her refusal to abide by cultural norms regarding respect for authority.[83] At meetings for the Market Men and Women Association, the state umbrella group for Lagos markets, she does not take part in the traditional ceremonies, which causes offense to older and more traditional members. Likewise, a market manager (who is in his seventies) asked to meet with the market leader (who is in her fifties) to discuss a dispute with tax officers, but she refused to meet; the market director responded by issuing a circular challenging her authority.

The market leader's weakness partly explains the problem of the street vendors. Yet the local government, which has the capacity to remove the street vendors and has its secretariat adjacent to the market, has refused to get involved because its chairman wants to destroy the market and build a multistory modern market. In addition, the local government receives illicit daily fees from the street vendors. Government officials are also aware that the market leader cannot mobilize traders to threaten or embarrass them. The market leader's requests for help from the Market Men and Women Association have fallen on deaf ears, as she has offended the group's leaders.

In most cases where the local government chairman has such desires and the market leader is weak, market renovation would have already happened by now. But because of the involvement of the traditional ruler, who has an interest in protecting the leases of his friends and family, this has not happened. Unhappy with their stymied renovation efforts, the local government has refused to force the street vendors to leave, hoping to put the market traders out of business. Indeed, this appears to be happening.

The case of Dabiri reveals that external threats are not a sufficient condition for private good governance. If the market leader were stronger – if her lease-holding divisions were less salient, or if she had no other businesses – she might have been motivated and able to mobilize traders to protest against the

---

[82] Interview with market manager C on September 26, 2014.
[83] Interview with market manager B on August 3, 2017.

street vendor situation at the state government secretariat. But because such mobilization is not feasible, she made calls to state government officials to complain about the street vendors, but the state officials made half-hearted attempts to get rid of them, such as sending people to remove them one day, only to have them return the next day. The market has not been able to demand that the government take more drastic action or send the street vendor removers more frequently. In short, the market's inability to threaten politicians impedes market order.

Dabiri happens to be under the jurisdiction of a local government that aims to intervene in organized societal groups. In 2014, when I started researching this market, the local government chairman was in his forties and ambitious. He was in his second term, and planning to run for a third. If he did not win, he aspired to run for state office. Either way, he aimed to increase the local government's internally generated revenue, a critical metric on which the patron of politics in Lagos state judges local government chairmen.

While it is theoretically plausible that politicians might be more likely to intervene in very profitable markets, I believe other forces more strongly influence their desire to intervene. Consistent with this hypothesis, the example of the Dabiri market shows that governments intervene in unprofitable markets as well. For example, local government officials come to Dabiri to collect a variety of fees, such as those related to putting up shop signs. Recently, frustrated with traders' unwillingness to pay these fees, the local government removed all signs, including the main market sign.[84]

This should somewhat assuage concerns of reverse causality. While more powerful market associations in this local government might be more successful at fending off government threats, I believe interventionist local governments *aim* to intervene in all markets under their jurisdiction.

Occasionally, the market leader has small successes in advocating for the interests of the traders. For example, she organized the traders to boycott a manager-initiated increase in electricity fees.[85] And "she promotes cleaning of the market to avoid eyes from local government."[86] This is an example of the logic of external threats motivating order: the market leader encourages overcoming a collective action problem (keeping the market clean) to avoid government intrusion. But overall, she lacks the strength to effectively push back against government threats.

As predicted by my theory, the weak leader in Dabiri is unable to mobilize traders. One trader could not think of a single time the market leader tried to mobilize traders.[87]

I similarly expect that, when leaders cannot mobilize traders, politicians will not visit the market to campaign. Indeed, traders report that politicians did not visit the market preceding the July 2017 local government elections.[88]

[84] Interview with trader K on July 31, 2017.
[85] Interviews with traders J and L on July 31, 2017.
[86] Interview with trader M on August 1, 2017.
[87] Interview with trader L on July 31, 2017.
[88] Interviews with traders J and L on July 31, 2017.

5.4 "OUR ASSOCIATION HERE NA FOR DECORATION": THE CASE OF DESTINY ASSOCIATION

The Destiny Association market is governed by weak leaders and does not face threats from the government. It is an association within a larger commercial area. When the commercial area was created in 1975,[89] the land was divided into sections in which certain products would be sold, and each section has its own association. Destiny Association was formed in 1978 for traders selling home wares, such as dishes and mugs.[90] Originally, the association was for traders from all ethnic groups.

Around 2000, there were disputes regarding who should head the association. A trader became head, but was toppled soon after. "There was chaos," according to a current market executive.[91] Following this crisis, the local government began involving itself in market affairs. "[The local government] observed that we did not have an elders council here," the market executive said, referencing an advisory board of senior traders that many markets have. "So [the local government] became a supervisor."[92] The local government divided the area into three associations: for the Igbo, for the Hausa, and for the Yoruba. Destiny Association became the association just for the Igbo traders.

Within the larger commercial area, Destiny Association has a desirable location close to the main road. Destiny Association's traders have makeshift shops called containers, because the material used to sell their products comes from shipping containers. Traders hang their wares from the metal sheets, which can be locked up in the evening.

Market leaders are elected to three-year terms, with two-term limits.[93] Traders believe the market leaders act independently and do not collude with the local government.[94]

5.4.1 Unengaged Market Leaders

The market association is characterized by in-fighting and unengaged market leaders. "Oh, our association here na for decoration," one trader told me.[95] In December 2016, thieves stole all of this trader's products, valued at N75,000 ($208). The trader reported this to the market leaders, who asked him to detail exactly what was stolen, which he did. The leaders promised to provide funds as partial compensation. The trader approached them repeatedly to follow up on this promise, but was never provided any compensation. The trader decided to stop paying the monthly "container fee" to the association, and the

---

[89] To protect the identity of the market, this is not the exact year.

[90] I have changed the product to protect the identity of the market. The products sold in this market are of similar value to home wares.

[91] Interview with market executive C on March 9, 2017.

[92] Interview with market executive C on March 9, 2017.

[93] Interviews with trader N on August 7, 2017, and trader O on August 15, 2017.

[94] Interview with trader O on August 15, 2017.

[95] Interview with trader P on February 24, 2017.

executives never made an issue out of this.[96] Nor did the leadership investigate how his goods were stolen.

The predictions for weak market leaders who do not face state threats of private predation are ambiguous. In this market association, it is not clear if there is predation, per se. The executives collect N500 ($1.39) to N1,500 ($4.17) per month from traders, and they appear to use at least some of this for electricity, security, and social functions. One trader believes the executives properly account for these fees. He says he sees the security guards doing their job – if the association was not paying them, they would have stopped coming.[97] Several traders disagree. One said there is "no financial transparency."[98] Another said, "there is not much financial probity," arguing that there has never been a meeting at which the market leaders disclose how the fees are spent.[99] In the 2015 survey, none of the five surveyed traders reported that the executives properly account for the fees they collect.

Destiny leaders provide few trade-promoting services. The leaders only warn traders not to buy stolen goods *in general*.[100] But when asked if the market executives ever shared information about particular dubious suppliers, a trader who belonged to the association since 2008 said that "has never happened."[101] Other traders agreed: the leaders do not share information about customers or suppliers.[102] Likewise, just one of the five surveyed traders said the market leaders shared information about customers and suppliers with traders.

The leaders provide a middling level of dispute-resolution services. When asked if the leaders would help out a trader who sold on credit to a customer who never repaid, one trader said they would only help if the customer was another trader who belonged to the association.[103] Then the executives might give the customer an ultimatum and potentially lock their shop. But if the customer was from outside the market association, the executives would not get involved: "That's for the trader and customer to settle."[104]

Another trader disagreed – the executives *do* get involved in disputes that involve individuals from outside Destiny Association, he said. He explained that support from the executives was one of the benefits of associational membership. "If you know them very well [they will side with you]," the trader said.[105] Only one trader responded that the executives had helped him resolve a dispute in the past year. It is clear that Destiny executives are not providing trade-promoting *impartial* dispute-resolution services.

---

[96] Interview with trader P on March 9, 2017.
[97] Interview with trader Q on February 28, 2017.
[98] Interview with trader N on August 7, 2017.
[99] Interview with trader O on August 15, 2017.
[100] Interview with executive D on February 28, 2017.
[101] Interview with trader P on February 24, 2017.
[102] Interviews with trader N on August 7, 2017, and trader O on August 15, 2017.
[103] Traders sometimes source from other traders in the same market.
[104] Interview with executive D on February 28, 2017.
[105] Interview with trader P on March 9, 2017.

When asked if the market executives represent the interests of traders, one trader said he couldn't say because he has not "really seen them in action."[106]

Yet the market is not governed by predatory leaders. The traders can point to some positive actions the leaders have taken. For example, the leaders organized with the local government to provide loans to traders and have taken some steps to promote security in the market.[107]

Security was the main issue discussed during the market leadership elections.[108] When the larger commercial area was first formed, the Hausa people were provided with three mosques and a space to trade. This area is adjacent to Destiny Association. Many sections of the market have gates around their association that get locked at night. But because some of the Hausa traders sleep in the mosques, it is not possible to have gates around Destiny Association. According to Destiny traders, this is why their association has problems related to theft.

One trader interprets the number of different associations as one reason why the executives have not been able to respond more effectively to the security situation. Because the Hausa traders have their own association, it is hard for all of the traders in this area to unite to address the security challenges. "Since they have three chairmen in [local term for the home wares area], it's hard to fix the security issue."[109]

5.4.2 Explaining the Absence of Trade-Promoting Policies in Destiny

Destiny Association leaders are weak. "Sadly it is not a well-organized association compared to other associations inside [this commercial area]," one trader said.[110]

Market meetings are held irregularly and are poorly attended, unless there is an emergency.[111] Traders are not required to attend, and one trader appeared to suggest that the executives do not want traders to attend the meetings. The executives try to make conversations at these meetings inaccessible. "You don't understand what is happening," one trader said. "They want to take care of issues behind closed doors."[112] In other markets in this commercial area, shops close for market meetings. That is not the case for Destiny Association.

The Destiny Association executives are permitted to lock up traders' shops, and they use this power occasionally when traders have not paid their association dues. However, their strength appears limited in this regard. "Some traders

---

[106] Interview with trader Q on February 28, 2017.
[107] Interview with trader O on August 15, 2017.
[108] Interview with executive C on March 9, 2017.
[109] Interview with trader S on February 28, 2017.
[110] Interview with trader P on March 9, 2017.
[111] Interviews with trader N on August 7, 2017, and trader O on August 15, 2017. Four of the five surveyed traders said that there were no regular meetings for traders.
[112] Interview with trader P on March 9, 2017.

are stubborn," one executive said. "They'll cut the padlock and continue doing business."[113]

Moreover, there are divisions within Destiny Association among the Igbo traders based on what state traders are from. The Anambra, Imo, and Enugu states are each represented. There has been "zoning" among these three states, a Nigerian term that indicates alternating power among subgroups. Each time Destiny holds elections, the state that the chairman comes from alternates. However, there are even divisions among the traders from a single state. For example, it was recently the turn of Igbo traders from Imo state to choose their candidate, but they could not agree on one, and the dispute turned violent. Traders brought cutlasses, machetes, and "traditional guns" to the market. Traders called police from different units (some from units near the market, and others from units where the traders live), which caused additional problems. Ultimately, the local government intervened and appointed one of the Imo candidates as temporary chairman.[114] The Imo people were supposed to be given the opportunity to pick their chairman again in the summer of 2017.

Destiny Association does not face meaningful state threats, primarily because the commercial area that it is a part of has its own umbrella association, which is responsible for "protecting the market from external aggression," according to a Destiny executive.[115] When the local government recently tried to increase the taxes that traders in this area had to pay – from N6,500 ($18) per year to N20,000 ($56) per year – it was the umbrella association that negotiated on the traders' behalf, not the Destiny executives.[116]

Now "there are no problems with the local government," one trader said.[117] In fact, the Destiny executives rarely even meet with local government officials.

In 2015, the Lagos state government was planning to relocate the entire commercial area far outside the city center. This was part of a broader master plan that would encompass relocating another commercial area as well. This threat did not motivate Destiny executives to govern well, in part because it was the *umbrella* association that organized a response. As of March 2017, the state government appears to have abandoned this plan.

When asked if there was any other government entity Destiny Association dealt with, no one interviewed could think of one.[118] "We hardly relate with

---

[113] Interview with executive D on February 28, 2017.

[114] Interview with trader P on March 9, 2017.

[115] Interview with executive C on March 9, 2017.

[116] The umbrella association succeeded in this regard, successfully making the case that, because of the depreciation of the naira, businesses were not profiting as much as they had before. As of March 2017, traders were still paying N6,500 ($18) per year.

[117] Interview with trader Q on February 28, 2017. Trader N said something similar on August 7, 2017.

[118] For example, interview with trader O on August 15, 2017.

TABLE 5.2 *Leader selection rules*

Market	Leaders elected?	Terms	Term limits
Oke Arin	Yes	4 years	None
Ebe Ebe	Yes	Position for life	NA
Dabiri	Yes	Position for life	NA
Destiny	Yes	3 years	2 terms

Notes: The four markets discussed in this chapter all have elected leaders, but their terms and term limits vary. These data come from a combination of interviews and survey data. The survey data included two traders from Oke Arin, eight traders from Ebe Ebe, five traders from Destiny, and four traders from Dabiri.

government agencies here," one trader said.[119] When asked about any issues with the government in general, traders complained about double taxation. Due to an unusual situation regarding the land they are on,[120] they pay taxes for their shops to the local government as well as land use fees to the Lagos state government; again, this is a threat that the umbrella association would deal with. Traders did not perceive any other serious threats from government. Overall, Destiny faces few government threats largely due to the presence of the umbrella association.

Given the weakness of the market leaders, it is not surprising that traders cannot remember ever being mobilized by their leaders.[121] Politicians do visit the market,[122] but this is likely because the broader commercial area has thousands of traders. Politicians do not appear to visit Destiny market leaders in particular.

5.5 ALTERNATIVE SOURCES OF MARKET GOOD GOVERNANCE

These four markets have illustrated how external threats can motivate private leaders to promote trade, and how, in the absence of such threats, group leaders may extort from their members. In this section I discuss the plausibility of explanations related to the time horizon of the market leader and the ethnic composition of the market, and I address questions about whether traders can sanction predatory market leaders and why traders would join a badly governed market in the first place.

5.5.1 Time Horizon

What role does the leader's time horizon play in explaining market leader governance? Mancur Olson has seminally argued that a leader's time horizon affects the likelihood of private good governance: when a leader has a long time horizon, she will be motivated to protect group members from outside

---

[119] Interview with trader N on August 7, 2017.
[120] Expanding on this would make the market identifiable.
[121] Interview with trader N on August 7, 2017.
[122] Interviews with trader N on August 7, 2017, and trader O on August 15, 2017.

predatory actors, and not to extort (1993). She will want group members to be productive so as to maximize long-term tax collection.

There are some reasons to think this logic should play out in Lagos markets. Market leaders collect fees from traders that they sometimes pocket. Thus, if a market generates more business, market leaders could pocket more fees from traders.

The evidence from the cases, however, is not consistent with this theory. The Ebe Ebe market leader has a long time horizon; the leader is elected, but then holds his position for life. Yet the Ebe Ebe leader extorts from his own traders, and there is no evidence that he works to protect traders from local government extortion. The Oke Arin and Destiny markets, which span the range of governance quality, have rules stipulating regularly held elections.

The case of Dabiri sheds additional theoretical light on this question. Elinor Ostrom has theorized that a long time horizon might not be sufficient to motivate good private governance (1990). A leader may have other businesses, which could complicate the alignment of leader–member preferences that is theorized to arise with long time horizons. Indeed, this is the case in Dabiri. As noted earlier, the Dabiri leader holds the position for life, but she has several other businesses besides her shop in the market, one of which is a restaurant. Her restaurant might have greater growth potential, incentivizing her to focus on managing it and spending little time in the market. She currently intervenes little in market affairs. No trader I spoke with could recall a time when she was called on to resolve a dispute between a supplier and a trader, mostly because she is only rarely at the market, often tending to her other businesses.

5.5.2 Market Association Ethnic Composition

What if market association governance can be explained by the ethnic diversity of the market traders? Perhaps more homogenous markets are more cooperative, which results in the selection of better market leaders. The expectation would thus be that Oke Arin would be homogenous and the remaining three diverse. Yet data from the market cases, as seen in Table 5.3, do not provide strong support for this.

Ethnic homogeneity does not necessarily produce a sense of shared identity. Destiny Association illustrates this clearly: 95 percent of its traders are from

TABLE 5.3 *Market diversity*

Market	Igbo	Yoruba	Hausa and other
Oke Arin	85%	10%	5%
Ebe Ebe	70%	15%	15%
Dabiri	46%	44%	10%
Destiny	95%	3%	2%

Notes: Some of the markets are more ethnically diverse than others, but this is not associated with private governance. Source: Trader estimates from interviews.

the Igbo ethnic group, but there are divisions *among* the Igbo traders based on what state they are from, as well as among traders from the same state. Therefore, even "homogenous" markets can have disruptive divisions.

What if the ethnic domination of the market leadership explains the association's governance? Perhaps having a market leadership with representatives from many ethnic groups would be good for governance, but at the same time such institutions seem equally likely to be a function of good governance. Perhaps ethnic representation in leadership only matters in more diverse markets.

In Oke Arin and Destiny, traders perceive that the Igbos dominate the market leadership.[123] The Dabiri market leadership simply consists of a single leader who is Yoruba. Ebe Ebe is an interesting case. Prior to the market's renovation, it had mostly Yoruba traders and Yoruba leadership. But since the renovation and subsequent increased rental prices, the market has become mostly Igbo. But because the market rules stipulate that leaders hold their position for life, its leader remains Yoruba. This could be contributing to the market's problems, though evidence from the other markets suggests that the ethnic composition of the market leadership was less relevant.

5.5.3 Sanctioning

To what extent can traders sanction the behavior of predatory market leaders? There is limited evidence of this taking place. In Oke Arin, a treasurer for one section of the market lost his position for not accounting properly for fees. While traders had complained to the market-wide leaders about the improper behavior of this line leader, it was the main market leadership who ultimately removed the treasurer. So, to the extent that this is an example of sanctioning, it illustrates sanctioning with the support of the market leadership.[124]

In Ebe Ebe, all of the interviewed traders expressed frustration with the market leaders. Indeed, they had once united in an attempt to sanction the leader's behavior. Specifically, they worked to negotiate lower market fees and a reduced parking fee, which they felt was deterring customers. The latter attempt was somewhat successful: the executives dropped the parking fee from N200 ($0.56) to N100 ($0.28). When the traders asked the leaders to lower the market fees, however, the leaders summoned them to a meeting and threatened to raise the fees further. "They did it like a game so that we the traders won't ask for reduction again."[125]

In general, across markets, traders do not come together to try to lobby the market leaders. "Everyone is doing his or her own thing," one Ebe Ebe trader explained.[126] In Dabiri and Destiny, no trader could think of an example of

---

[123] Interviews with traders E and F on August 1, 2017, and trader H on August 3, 2017.
[124] Interview with trader H on August 3, 2017.
[125] Interview with trader A on August 1, 2017.
[126] Interview with trader B on August 1, 2017.

traders attempting to sanction leader behavior. "It is a hard thing to do," one Destiny trader said.[127]

5.5.4 Why Not Leave Badly Governed Markets? And Why Join in the First Place?

What is preventing traders in Dabiri, Destiny, and Ebe Ebe from relocating to a different market? There are three main factors. First, advance rent is the norm in Lagos, as in many cities in the developing world. Traders must typically pay two years of rent upfront to rent a shop, and one year in advance thereafter, which represents a huge amount of money and greatly disincentivizes relocation. Second, perhaps in part due to political uncertainty in Nigeria more generally, there is often hope that conditions in a market will improve.

Third, prior to joining a market, a trader has imperfect information about conditions in the market. Dabiri is unequivocally an undesirable market to trade in, yet, while conducting research there, I met three women who were submitting their documents to lease a shop there. All of the traders interviewed in 2017 were asked whether they had any information about market leader governance prior to joining the market, and they all said they did not. Traders reported choosing to rent shops in certain markets because it was the market they apprenticed in,[128] was close to their home (or otherwise in a desirable location),[129] or was cheap to rent.[130]

Why don't the traders join together and start up their own new market? This would seem an especially attractive option in Ebe Ebe, given that opposition to the market leader was widespread. Starting a new market, though, would be exceptionally difficult. Space in Lagos – the most densely populated city in Africa[131] – is tight.

While one might think these constraints are specific to markets in Lagos, sorting into new groups is costly in most contexts. For example, if an individual belongs to an electrician association, there is unlikely to be another such association nearby to join if they are dissatisfied with the current one. Starting a new association could be tricky for many reasons, since the current association may be the recognized group for negotiating with the municipal government. Many private associations, such as slum development committees in India, are registered with the government (Auerbach, 2017). Lobbying the government to negotiate with an additional association might not be straightforward.

Sheilagh Ogilvie has highlighted a related, persistent source of inefficient institutions: institutional change is a collective action problem (2004). Everyone would benefit from institutional improvement, but the benefits would be

---

[127] Interview with trader O on August 15, 2017.
[128] Interview with trader O on August 15, 2017.
[129] Interviews with trader J on July 31, 2017, and traders A and D on August 1, 2017.
[130] Interviews with trader K on July 31, 2017, and trader M on August 1, 2017.
[131] See, for example, citymayors.com/statistics/largest-cities-density-125.html.

diffuse. Meanwhile, even if the costs of change would be small, they would be concentrated among group leaders.

5.6 CONCLUSION

While Edward Stringham states that "the more seamless private governance is, the fewer people notice it or appreciate its beauty. Private governance is so often missed" (2015, p. 8), I disagree. There is an abundance of research on effective private governance focused on groups that resemble Oke Arin, the case of private good governance. This leads to the incorrect assumption that private governance is ubiquitous, when in fact groups like Ebe Ebe, Dabiri, and Destiny abound. Private good governance should thus be considered unusual, and its presence must be explained.

Disorderly groups can be hard to see; a customer cheated in such a market might be unable to find a leader to whom they wish to complain, as perhaps the leader is rarely at the market. The customer – or researcher – could then incorrectly assume that the group lacks leadership. This is the challenge for scholars of private group governance. In Chapter 6, I will compare a larger set of markets that – as in this chapter – have different governance institutions. I will assess whether the relationship between threats and good governance holds for the larger sample and examine the relationship between within-group competition and private pro-trade policies.

6

Business is Secret: Government Threats and Within-Group Competition

Chapter 5 examined four market associations in depth, showing how strong and weak market associations responded to government threats, and what happened in the absence of these threats. That chapter built on prior work on private governance, which often focuses on case studies of groups with sophisticated institutions that promote trade. Three of the four market associations were badly governed, with either predatory leaders or with those who did little at all.

I expect that within-group competition should make it more difficult for group leaders to obtain information from traders about their business partners, and harder to mobilize them in general. Market leader efforts to sanction politicians will be frustrated when traders in their market sell similar products, and are thus in competition with each other. It will be easier to mobilize traders and promote intra-market collaboration when traders sell different products and are not in direct competition. Market traders sometimes appear to be very friendly with other traders near their shop. While this may occasionally be the case, or traders may be friendly with each other in some ways, the relationships are frequently uncooperative and secretive. I heard a story of a shoe trader stealing another shoe trader's passport to prevent him from traveling to China to buy shoes. Traders also mentioned that they sometimes find a neighbor's shop locked unexpectedly, indicating that they likely traveled in secret to make purchases.

A cell phone accessory trader once told me he had never heard of his association organizing collective boycotts against dubious suppliers. "Why? Because people keep who they work with a secret. I don't want to tell other people here who I am buying things from," he said. A jeans and shirts seller I met would also never tell people about his suppliers. "That's my own secret." The other traders on the same floor of his plaza go so far as to use separate travel agents because they do not want others to know when they are traveling. One constantly hears the phrase "business is secret" in Lagos, and many traders say they are reluctant to cooperate with other traders in their market because "they are my competitors" or someone might "snatch my customers." When levels of competition are high, market leaders will be frustrated in their efforts to implement trade-promoting policies and mobilize traders against government threats.

In this chapter I first test the main premise of the project – that external threats should make private trade-promoting policies more likely – using a large sample of markets. I evaluate whether the data are consistent with the notion that leaders enact such policies in order to maintain their ability to mobilize traders against government threats. Next, I assess whether (and how) competition mediates the role of these threats. Just as important, I can use these data to assess alternative explanations that have been posited but rarely tested in the context of private governance with a sample of this size.

The key finding is that markets facing government threats – that is, those on local government land[1] – are more likely to be governed well. Prior work and conventional wisdom would lead one to expect that, especially in a place like Nigeria where local politicians have a reputation for being corrupt and predatory, threats of government intervention should be associated with worse private governance. Consistent with my argument, none of the findings supports that contention. This relationship between land type and private governance, however, is not uniform. It depends on the diversity of products sold in a market. Public land markets are governed better when they sell a variety of products, since traders are in less direct competition with each other.

This chapter has important implications for theories of private governance. It highlights the significant role that competition plays in impeding the implementation of trade-promoting policies, and helps to explain when – and why – collectively beneficial institutions will emerge.

6.1 DATA

To the best of my knowledge, I am the first to measure market leader governance. I am not aware of any similar trader-level surveys that identify associational membership, let alone ask about leader governance. I developed survey questions to assess the quality of leader governance based on a year of my own qualitative interviews with traders, asking which services they consider to be important. I used their own phrases and terms in the surveys to assess how the leaders govern. (In Chapter 3 I described how I collected the survey data. Appendix D.1 lists the survey questions.) For example, imagine a market that has parking spaces for customers, but employees from a neighboring bank park in these spots. A precise way to measure leader governance would be to ask whether the market leader is working to prevent bank

---

[1] I determined that this was the most common type of external threat facing markets based on my interviews. However, markets do face other threats. Chapter 5, for example, discussed how the possibility of intervention from the National Agency for Food and Drug Administration and Control was a relevant external threat for the Oke Arin market. The surveys could not capture the universe of state threats that these markets face.

employees from taking the parking spots designated for market customers. But as I lacked prior information about the specific challenges facing each market, more general questions were the second-best option. These questions were designed to differentiate between market leaders who work to promote an environment conducive to trade and those who take a laissez-faire or even predatory approach to market governance.

I look at four measures of market leader good governance. I use questions that can be interpreted consistently across associations. Traders were asked whether the market leaders represent their interests, which is the closest approximation to trade-supporting policies in the absence of data on the particular issues facing each market. Private extortion is used here to denote market leaders' extortion of traders, which I assess using a low-measurement-error question: whether traders feel market leaders *properly account for the fees they collect*. I developed this question by listening to the language traders use to talk about market leader management. Leaders who, for example, collect fees for electricity but pocket these funds would not be accounting properly. Traders were also asked whether they feel free to complain to market leaders in order to evaluate leader accessibility. Last, traders were asked if their market leaders had helped them resolve any disputes with other traders in the past year.

Markets like Oke Arin would score high on each component, and those such as Ebe Ebe would score the lowest. Markets like Dabiri, which has a laissez-faire leader, would be somewhere in the middle: traders reported that they feel free to complain to her, but she never helps to resolve disputes.

The primary explanatory factors are land and product diversification – the measure of competition. Traders were asked what type of land their market association was on. I created a product diversification index for market associations for which I have data from at least five traders. The index is based on the number of traders selling products categorized as apparel, electronics, beauty, hardware, or home goods.[2] A higher score indicates higher diversification, that is, traders are selling a wider variety of products.

I control for factors that might affect assessments of market leaders' governance. First, I include a control variable indicating whether the market leader holds their position for life; Mancur Olson (2000) theorizes that a long time horizon may be sufficient to align the incentives of the leader and group members. Indeed, if group leaders seek to maximize their income, which is a function of the fees collected from group members proportional to the amount of wealth generated in the group, greater group order seems likely to increase group-derived leader profits over the long term. However, a long time horizon may not be sufficient to constrain short-term temptations to extort. Leaders can have conflicts of interest, such as other businesses and income streams, that may encourage them to exploit short-term opportunities at the expense of

---

[2] This index sums the squares of the proportion of traders selling in these product categories, and subtracts that value from one.

the group's long-term revenue growth (Ostrom, 1990). Additionally, it is often difficult to predict the length of a leader's tenure, since this may be influenced by high levels of political uncertainty and events beyond their control such as natural and human-influenced disasters. Yet this is still an important variable to account for in the models.

Additionally, I control for whether the trader has any postsecondary education, how many employees he or she has, and the total value of the trader's stock.[3] I also include local government fixed effects.

I measure market political engagement in two ways. First, traders were asked whether the market leader provides them with political information. Second, traders were asked if they had ever slept in their shop the night before an election so they could vote in the local government district where they trade. In Nigeria, vehicle movement is prohibited on election day, and many traders live and work in different districts. Politically engaged market leaders will mobilize traders to sleep in their shops on the eve of elections so they can vote in the market's constituency.[4]

6.2 EVIDENCE

In March 2017 I met with executives at a Lagos state government agency that provides loans to microenterprises. While discussing loan repayment, I asked if market leaders ever helped to secure loan payments from traders. "In our experience, associations in general are useless," an official said. "When you meet with them, at first they tell you they will help you recover funds [...]. But then they don't in practice. In [a commercial area, one of the associations] said they would help, but push come to shove they didn't. The only association that has really helped with this is [the Computer and Allied Product Dealers Association of Nigeria – a market association in a commercial area called Computer Village]."[5] This statement supports the theoretical expectation that market associations will not necessarily implement trade-promoting policies. Due to the costs to leaders of sustaining such policies, I did not expect them to be common. Indeed, this is what the survey data suggest.

The modal trader reports that the market leader only "sometimes" represents their interests (mean, 0.63) and has not helped them resolve disputes recently (mean, 0.37). However, the modal trader also reports that their leader accounts honestly for fees (mean, 0.76), and that they feel free to complain to them (mean, 0.92). This suggests that, as expected, the costliest trade-promoting services such as dispute resolution are rare, and that market leaders are not always working in the interest of traders. The higher scores for honest accounting suggest that predatory leaders are less common.

---

3 Theoretically, the number of employees and stock value could be a result of market leader governance – that is, good governance might help traders grow their businesses. Removing these controls does not meaningfully change the results. See Grossman (2020) for these results.

4 Chapter 2 discussed the significance of shop sleeping in greater detail.

5 Interview with Lagos state government official A on March 14, 2017.

Overall, these statistics suggest that laissez-faire governance is common, and that exceptionally good and predatory governance is present, but not ubiquitous.

In the analyses that follow, I use ordinary least squares regressions, clustering standard errors at the market association level, to examine the relationship between leader policies and the type of land the market is on, and competition.[6]

6.2.1   Hypothesis 1a: Markets on Local Government Land Are Governed Better

What is the relationship between the type of land a market is on and the quality of market leader governance? Table 6.1 shows that markets located on local government land are better governed and are more vulnerable to government threats. The predicted representativeness score for markets on private land is 0.60, and for those on government land is 0.73.[7] The predicted honest accounting score for markets on private land is 15 percent lower than for those on government land – 0.75 versus 0.88.[8]

These findings are especially striking, given that markets on local government land are typically based in areas zoned exclusively for markets. One might expect badly governed markets to be most likely located on land that cannot be used for any other purpose. But markets on government land face more threats of politician interference, and, as Table 6.1 shows, private good governance is more likely in these markets.

I find no relationship between the type of land ownership and whether traders report feeling free to complain to their leaders. I suspect this is because there is little variation in this variable: 92 percent of traders reported that they feel free to complain to their leaders. Nor is there any connection between land type and whether the market leader actively tries to resolve disputes in the market, except in the model with controls. Disputes are a complicated variable to interpret, as their absence could indicate reliable market leader governance: they may never arise in the first place. Alternatively, they could suggest that traders trust the market leader and are bringing more disputes to him or her.

The ability to incorporate local government fixed effects is a powerful feature of the research design. A possible criticism is that it is variation *across* local governments that is driving the relationship. For example, some local governments may intervene in all markets in their jurisdiction to protect traders from abusive leaders. Models 2 and 4 show that the surprising correlation holds even for the relationship between leader good governance and land type *within*

---

[6] Appendix D.3 shows descriptive statistics. In Appendix D.4 I assess whether we should be concerned that traders are nervous about speaking openly about predatory market leaders.

[7] Model 2.

[8] These results are robust to excluding observations not included in the models with controls, subsetting to market associations for which I have data from at least two traders, and subsetting to market associations for which I have data from at least five traders. See the Appendix of Grossman (2020) for these tables.

TABLE 6.1 This table shows the relationship between land type and private good governance. The sample size changes across models due to missing data. Controls include whether the market leader holds her position for life, whether the trader has any postsecondary education, the number of employees the trader has, and the value of stock in a trader's shop. LGA fixed effects indicate the inclusion of local government fixed effects. Standard errors are clustered at the market association level.

	Dependent variable:							
	Represent		Honest accounting		Free to complain		Resolve dispute	
	(1)	(2)	(3)	(4)	(5)	(6)	(7)	(8)
Local government land	0.10*	0.10**	0.15***	0.10**	0.002	0.02	0.06	0.10**
	(0.05)	(0.04)	(0.05)	(0.05)	(0.04)	(0.04)	(0.05)	(0.05)
Constant	0.61***	0.73**	0.73***	0.85***	0.92***	0.85***	0.36***	0.53**
	(0.03)	(0.33)	(0.03)	(0.29)	(0.02)	(0.24)	(0.02)	(0.25)
Observations	670	640	519	498	674	642	699	664
Controls	No	Yes	No	Yes	No	Yes	No	Yes
LGA fixed effects	No	Yes	No	Yes	No	Yes	No	Yes

Note: *p<0.1; **p<0.05; ***p<0.01

local governments. Moreover, my fieldwork suggests that no local government acts in this way.

An additional concern is that leaders treat individual traders within their market association differently. This is a downside to the model I use, which is an individual analysis with standard errors clustered at the market association level. To address this concern, as a robustness check I also aggregate variables at the market association level and conduct an ordinary least squares regression using this smaller sample. The results generally remain the same.[9]

To illustrate the spectrum of private governance, we can compare market associations with these predicted scores. For instance, a market association of traders selling electrical supplies has an average representativeness score of 0.74 and an average honest accounting score of 0.86. When asked how the market executives advocate for the traders in this market, one trader said, "the executives make sure they frustrate dubious suppliers who supply substandard goods to traders [and] help traders recover debt." Another trader said, "they give proper account of our money." And one trader said, "they make policy that prevents marketers from been disturbed by outsiders." A market association with traders who primarily sell footwear scored 0.59 on representativeness and 0.75 on honest accounting. A trader from this association said the leaders "don't advocate for our interests." The leaders of this market do not sound predatory, but instead focused on more basic and social functions. One trader said, if a group member dies, the association will give money to the family. Another trader said the association provides identification cards to traders, which helps them buy from manufacturers. There was no mention of the more sophisticated policies suggested by traders in the electrical supplies market.[10] In short, the differences in the predicted values from Models 2 and 4 of Table 6.1 are substantively meaningful.

6.2.1.1   *Hypothesis 1b: Product Diversification*

Table 6.2 considers the interaction between land type and the diversity of products sold in the market. Models 1 and 2 provide strong support for my theory. The interaction between private land and product diversification is negative and large, suggesting that the relationship between threats (being on local government land) and private good governance is greater when markets sell a wide variety of goods, presumably because traders are in less competition with each other. This makes it easier for market leaders to implement trade-promoting policies.

The markets that perform best on the good governance measures are those located on public land with a high product diversification index – the predicted value of representativeness for markets on local government land with a product diversification score one standard deviation below and above the mean is 0.47 compared to 0.75. Greater product diversification helps private land

---

[9] See Grossman (2020) for the results of this analysis.

[10] These responses come from the 2015 Lagos Trader Survey, which asked traders how their main market or plaza association advocates for their interests.

TABLE 6.2 *This table shows the interaction of land type and a market's product diversification index. A higher diversification index indicates that the market has traders selling a wider variety of products. The data for this table are subsetted to markets where there are five or more traders surveyed in the association. Standard errors are clustered at the market association level.*

	Dependent variable:			
	Represent (1)	Honest accounting (2)	Free to complain (3)	Resolve dispute (4)
Local government land	−0.05 (0.05)	−0.02 (0.07)	−0.10 (0.11)	0.12** (0.05)
Product diversification	0.27*** (0.09)	0.19 (0.13)	0.05 (0.08)	0.11 (0.07)
Local govt. land* product diversification	0.27** (0.11)	0.29* (0.15)	0.22 (0.19)	−0.21* (0.11)
Constant	0.52*** (0.03)	0.66*** (0.05)	0.89*** (0.02)	0.33*** (0.03)
Observations	477	359	472	494
Controls	No	No	No	No
LGA fixed effects	No	No	No	No

Note: *p<0.1; **p<0.05; ***p<0.01

markets too: the predicted value of representativeness increases from 0.52 to 0.66, moving between a standard deviation below and above the diversification mean. The same pattern holds for the honest accounting and free to complain variables, though the interaction effect for the latter is not statistically significant.

Because land is only a proxy for politician threats – after all, private land markets may also occasionally face such threats – I also examine the simple correlation between product diversification and good governance indicators. Diversification is associated with higher representativeness and honest accounting scores.[11]

Taken together, these results suggest that markets located on public land are more likely to have better private governance, and that greater product diversification enhances this relationship.

I expected product diversification to matter for its role in shaping competition among traders in an association. The data show that absolute levels of information sharing and other forms of cooperation are low. In the year prior to being surveyed, only 9 percent of traders reported ever discussing problems they were having with suppliers with other traders. While more than half reported giving or receiving a customer referral from a fellow trader, just 12 percent said they had ever given or received an introduction to a supplier or agent. And only 7 percent reported jointly sourcing their goods with another trader in the same order. When traders were asked why they may choose *not* to discuss supplier troubles with other traders, a third responded that they did not want other traders to know their private information.[12]

More than half of traders stated that they do not know any other trader who buys from their main overseas supplier. When asked how many other people they know who they could ask for advice about finding new suppliers or products, the average response was two. When asked how many other people they know who they could ask for advice about taxes, fees, or other business issues in Lagos – less sensitive information – the average response was just one.[13] In markets, secrecy appears to thrive.

6.2.2 Hypothesis 2: Is Market Political Engagement Associated with Leader Good Governance?

I have proposed that one way in which politician threats promote good governance is that leaders need traders' support to fend off these threats. If a leader extorts from his or her traders, he or she will not be able to mobilize them for political ends, such as encouraging them to vote as a bloc. One implication of this argument is that all politically active markets – irrespective of land type – should be better governed. After all, politicians will have little interest in markets with leaders who cannot mobilize traders to vote as a bloc.

---

[11] See Grossman (2020) for details.

[12] These data came from the third round of the Lagos Trader Survey in 2018.

[13] These data come from the second round of the Lagos Trader Survey in 2016.

TABLE 6.3 *This table shows the relationship between different measures of political engagement and market leader good governance. Standard errors are clustered at the market association level.*

	Dependent variable:							
	Represent		Honest accounting		Free to complain		Resolve dispute	
	(1)	(2)	(3)	(4)	(5)	(6)	(7)	(8)
Election info	0.11***		0.06		−0.003		0.21***	
	(0.03)		(0.05)		(0.03)		(0.04)	
Sleep		0.17***		0.16***		−0.01		0.14*
		(0.04)		(0.04)		(0.04)		(0.08)
Constant	0.59***	0.64***	0.75***	0.79***	0.93***	0.94***	0.28***	0.40***
	(0.03)	(0.03)	(0.03)	(0.03)	(0.02)	(0.01)	(0.03)	(0.02)
Observations	614	542	488	432	625	547	639	562
Controls	No	No	No	No	No	No	No	No
LGA fixed effects	No	No	No	No	No	No	No	No

Note: *$p<0.1$; **$p<0.05$; ***$p<0.01$

Table 6.3 examines the relationship between two measures of market political engagement and leader good governance: predicted representativeness and honest accounting. There is some suggestive evidence that markets with leaders who engage in two specific activities – providing traders with information about politicians and asking traders to sleep in their shops on election eve – are better governed. The predicted representativeness and honest accounting scores for markets where the leader does *not* ask traders to sleep in their shops before an election are 0.64 and 0.79, respectively. These increase to 0.81 and 0.95, respectively, for leaders who ask traders to sleep in their shops on election eve. These patterns hold for the dispute-resolution variable as well. It is possible that there is no relationship between these forms of political engagement and traders reporting being free to complain to their market leader given the small amount of variation in responses to that question.

6.2.3 Sources of Exogenous Variation

In this section I address concerns that omitted variables may be shaping both exposure to threats and the outcome, and that government threats might not be exogenous to the outcome. One concern is that well-governed markets may also be more prosperous than their poorly governed counterparts, and that this attracts local government attention and threats to their market. This is a difficult possibility to address empirically, as I expect well-governed markets to be better able to negotiate with the local government, which makes it difficult to observe threats toward these markets in equilibrium. However, there is generally no relationship between the good governance indicators and the total value of traders' stock;[14] nor is there a correlation between stock value and market land type. This suggests that local government threats are not targeted only at more prosperous markets, though it is difficult to fully address this endogeneity concern.

Another concern is that markets on public land are different from those on private land not *just* because of exposure to government threats, but in other ways that could directly affect market leader policies. For example, if these markets have different degrees of ethnic homogeneity, previous studies suggest that could explain the outcome. I test for this possibility by conducting a difference-in-means test for private and public land markets by level of ethnic fractionalization; there is no statistically significant difference. The main results are also robust to controlling for ethnic fractionalization, as described in Section 6.2. Similarly, there is no difference across public and private land markets in whether the leader holds their position for life (Table D.1), and the

---

[14] This finding is itself surprising, as I would have expected good governance to help traders grow their business. One possibility is that stock value is only distally related to market governance. Perhaps if the survey had asked about more proximate trade outcomes, such as how often customers buy on credit and fail to repay, I would have observed a relationship. There is a negative relationship between stock value and dispute resolution, but as noted later I do not put much weight on the dispute-resolution variable.

main results are virtually unchanged when controlling for whether the market leader holds their position for life (Table 6.1).

An additional concern is that private good governance may be more likely on public land markets *not* due to threats of politician interference, but because public markets sell high-end products or have more desirable locations, and the gains from pro-trade policies are therefore greater. I have already shown that the total value of a trader's stock does not differ across public or private land, which could proxy for product value. To assess location, I can compare shop rents across public and private land markets. Rents are about 26 percent *higher* in private land markets, which would increase the bar for finding an effect.

My theory predicts that a shift in exposure to politician threats or the diversity of products sold in a market could lead to changes in the nature of private governance. In the context studied here, land rarely shifts from being public to private, or vice versa. Some traders do, however, change the products they sell. I have panel data for 292 traders who were (1) surveyed in 2015, (2) included in the analysis in this chapter (i.e., those for whom I have associational membership data), (3) surveyed again in 2016, and (4) surveyed for a third time in 2018. Data from these traders suggest that traders who sell apparel, electronics, and hardware are unlikely to change the products they sell over the years, while traders who sell home goods and beauty products are highly likely to switch products. Future research could be designed to carefully assess whether traders respond to different forms of private governance by changing the types of products they sell. But given the path dependencies of land type, along with a smaller sample size in the panel, the empirical tests of the argument use cross-sectional data to assess expectations about leader governance given land type and product diversification at a given point in time.

A related endogeneity concern is that traders sort into markets based on the quality of market governance. Section 6.3 considers the evidence on trader sorting and concludes that it is extremely difficult for potential group members to learn about conditions within a market association before they join.

In short, while I believe land type provides a source of exogenous variation in the extent to which markets face government threats, there are likely to be some unusual situations in which threats are a function of market attributes that are unrelated to land. My strongest claim is that there is a surprising pattern – a correlation between markets located on public land (which is closely tied to threats of political interference) and private, pro-trade policies. Previous studies would predict the opposite. The empirical correlation is consistent with my argument, but I cannot definitively rule out the possibility of reverse causation.

6.3 ASSESSING ALTERNATIVE EXPLANATIONS OF PRIVATE GOVERNANCE

In this section I examine several alternative explanations of private good governance. First, I consider variables that have been shown to affect group cooperation, such as whether traders are embedded in each other's lives.

I define two traders as socially embedded if they live in the same local government constituency, which I determined using a residential dispersion index.[15] This variable mediates the relationship between land and good governance. Among markets comprising traders who live in different districts, private land markets are better governed than public land markets – 0.53 versus 0.41, respectively, on the representativeness index. Among markets in which traders live closer together, public land markets are better governed – 0.74 versus 0.69, respectively. Similar patterns hold for the honest accounting variable, but it is not clear what conclusions can be drawn from this finding, given that local government districts in Lagos have over 435,000 residents on average, so it is not obvious that traders would have higher social capital simply because they live in the same district. The dispersion concept merits further examination: future survey questions could investigate whether traders attend the same church or mosque in order to better assess whether they consider themselves part of the same community.

Four other variables might also affect traders' ability to act collectively: the size and ethnic homogeneity of market associations, product type, and geographical distance from the local government secretariat. First, smaller associations may be better able to cooperate, as Mancur Olson suggests (1965). The results hold when controlling for the size of the market association.[16] Second, the results also hold when controlling for an ethnic fractionalization index;[17] the coefficient on ethnic fractionalization is negative and large, suggesting that ethnic diversity is associated with worse private governance. Given that many markets are homogenous and badly governed, I did not expect ethnic homogeneity to be so strongly correlated with market association good governance, though several prior studies on this topic have predicted a strong relationship. So while ethnic homogeneity may not be sufficient for good governance, it *is* associated with better private governance, which is consistent with the existing literature.

Third, private good governance may be more critical for certain *types* of products, which may drive the provision of private pro-trade policies. Appendix D.3 provides evidence that private land markets may be more likely to sell electronics, and that markets on public land may be more likely to sell beauty products. It is not obvious, however, how this would matter. If anything, electronic products might be expected to benefit more from market leader governance, as it is harder to assess their quality on the spot.

---

[15] This variable is calculated in the same way as the product diversification index – by summing the squares of the proportion of traders residing in each local government district and subtracting that value from one.

[16] Market size is measured with a question from the second round of the panel survey, where enumerators asked traders how many of them belonged to their association. The coefficient on market size is not statistically significant, but I caution against putting too much weight on this finding given that the question was not asked in the same year as the other questions analyzed in this chapter.

[17] This variable is calculated as mentioned earlier – summing the squares of the proportion of traders belonging to each ethnic group, and subtracting that value from one.

Additionally, there is no relationship between the proportion of traders selling these product categories and market good governance.

Fourth, the distance between the market and the local government secretariat (a proxy for government threat) may matter since markets closer to the government could be more vulnerable to politician intrusion. However, I expect this factor to matter less in urban settings with small local government districts. And indeed, the results hold when controlling for this distance.

Market Sorting Is Difficult and Rare

If a leader is extorting heavily from group members, why wouldn't the members simply switch groups? Wouldn't this constrain extortion? This would seem to be especially true in the case at hand: traders' shops are quite small, and a trader could pack all of their wares into a taxi in an hour at most. Capital mobility should provide group members with more bargaining power vis-à-vis their leaders (Bates and Lien, 1985). In Section 3.4 I argued that group member sorting – that is, members identifying orderly groups and choosing to join them – should be difficult and rare. Here I examine the evidence.

An important obstacle to switching markets is that shop owners require two years' rent upfront from traders, which is the norm in Lagos (and many other West African cities) for residential leases as well. After these first two years, traders need only pay the following year's rent upfront, which deters relocation, as a new lease would require a further two years' rent in advance. Two years of advance rent is $4,585 for the average trader, which is 8 percent of two years of revenue.[18] The average trader in my sample had been in their market or plaza for over seven years.

It may be difficult to relocate, but can traders sort into trade-supporting markets in the first place? Table 6.1 shows that many traders were attracted to their plaza because it had a reputation for being a place where goods sold quickly; several chose a location based on reasons unrelated to whether the market leader maintained pro-trade policies. For example, 10 percent of traders reported being attracted to their plaza *only* because of its desirable location – for example, situated in a busy area, close to their home, or near their suppliers. Likewise, 9 percent of respondents reported being attracted to their plaza *only* because the product they sell was sold there.[19]

The fact that many traders select a market based on non-trade-related characteristics is at least partly because nonmembers have imperfect information about internal market affairs. Even diligent traders will struggle to obtain reliable information about conditions in a market they are considering joining. One trader tries to do her own survey of traders before renting a shop. "But most times, even if the market is bad, they won't tell her," her son said. "And if

---

[18] This calculation relies on Meredith Startz's estimate of trader revenue, which is drawn from the same survey data used here (2018).

[19] Note that Figure 6.1 shows all responses to the "check all that apply" question.

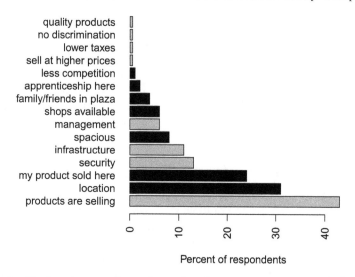

FIGURE 6.1 **Traders choose to locate in markets for many reasons, several of which are unrelated to whether the market is conducive to trade.** This figure shows responses to the question: "What attracted you to this plaza?" This was an open response question that was then coded. Gray bars denote reasons that could be related to market conditions, while black bars indicate unrelated reasons. The data come from a 2015 pilot for the survey (N = 196).

they know she wants to sell similar goods, they would even hoard information from her."[20]

Additionally, there is no relationship between association representativeness and honest accounting on the one hand, and how long a trader has been in their market on the other hand. Traders in the most and least representative associations report having been in their market for the same number of years: 7.6. This suggests that, at minimum, relocation is not frictionless.

6.3.1 No Evidence of Market Good Governance Clustering

Two separate logics lead to the prediction that well-governed associations might cluster together geographically. The first is that leaders may want to govern well but lack the know-how; thus, nearby leaders share information with each other about how to promote trade within their markets. On the one hand, this seems plausible, since umbrella associations could provide forums for group leaders to discuss their practices. On the other hand, I do not expect knowledge of good practices to be the primary constraint on private governance: it will be obvious to leaders that extorting from traders is harmful. Sharing information about dubious business partners takes effort, but I expect most group leaders know that it would be a useful service to provide.

---

[20] Interview with the son of a trader in Mile 12 market on June 13, 2016.

Additionally, my pre-survey fieldwork revealed no accounts of market leaders collaborating except in general local government-level meetings that included all market leaders in the area.

The second logic is that group leaders may be motivated to govern better in order to entice members to defect from other groups. I expect this to be unlikely, given the difficulty of acquiring reliable information about the quality of group governance prior to joining. But we can still test this hypothesis: if market leaders compete for traders, a given area might have similar levels of market governance.

The data support my intuition. Figure 6.2 shows the location of market associations on Lagos Island, a dense commercial area. Within this small area, the associations span the range of the representativeness variable.

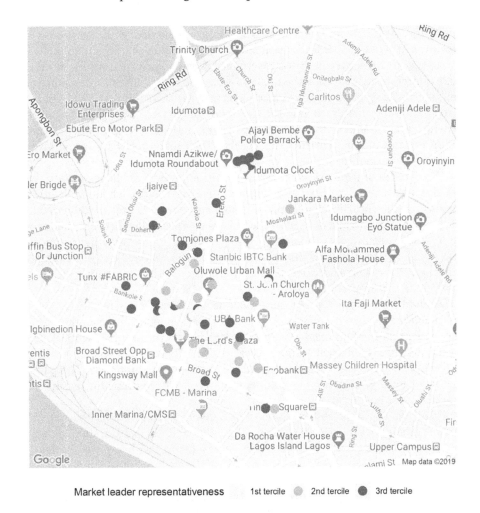

Market leader representativeness   1st tercile ○   2nd tercile ◐   3rd tercile ●

FIGURE 6.2 Market leader governance on Lagos Island
Notes: Each dot is a market association.

6.3.2 Does Variation in the Quality of Public Institutions Shape Private Governance?

My argument about the role of government interference in private groups is agnostic to the motivation behind the interference. The government could be interfering in order to predate, or to raise taxes that will be used to build a road. But what if the *quality* of the public institutional environment is more important? For instance, private predation could be less likely when the group is located in a jurisdiction with stronger and more impartial *public* institutions, since group members could bring complaints about group governance to politicians and bureaucrats. This may deter group leaders from predating.

However, when the quality of governance varies but is generally below a certain threshold,[21] the costs of inducing a government to force a leader to properly account for fees are very high, and the probability of success is uncertain. Moreover, it is not clear how being in a jurisdiction with a responsive government would make leader policies like information sharing more likely.

In general, when the quality of governance is higher, private institutions may be less important. Yet while the quality of national-level governance shapes a country's overall private governance expectations, even the best local politicians would be unable to provide the types of services that group leaders provide. For example, impartial courts might mitigate the need for private group policies like information sharing, but such institutions are beyond the control of local politicians.

Three pieces of evidence suggest that variation in local public institutions is not driving variation in market governance in Lagos. First, while public governance at the local level is improving in Lagos, traders still perceive local governments as corrupt. Indeed, traders do *not* perceive local governments to be representative. In a 2013 survey I asked traders what was the most important thing the local government had done for the market, and 60 percent said the government had done nothing significant. Other responses included services such as improving access to water and drainage.

Second, there is great variation in the quality of market association governance *within* local governments. A quarter of the 199 associations in the 2015 survey were in the Ojo local government jurisdiction. In six of these markets, all traders said the market leader represented their interests, while all traders in five of the markets said the leader did not represent their interests. Thus, the quality of local governance in Ojo does not appear to determine the quality of market leader governance.

Third, we can look at the relationship between market leader governance and the quality of governance in the local government district. Combining data from the 2012 Lagos State Household survey (2012) with my survey data,

---

[21] Afrobarometer public opinion data for African countries included in the 2016–2018 round shows that 49 percent strongly disapprove or disapprove of the performance of their elected local councilor, and 52 percent trust their elected local government council not at all or just a little.

I found no relationship between the percentage of individuals who reported that their local government is effective at service delivery and how well the market leader governs.

6.4 CONCLUSION

Prior research on private governance is largely based on case studies of groups that have sophisticated private governance institutions; it generally overlooks badly governed groups. In this chapter I assessed individual- and group-level data from a survey of traders in markets with different types of governing policies. This allowed me to test theories about the conditions that make pro-trade institutions more or less likely, which the case study approach is less equipped to do.

Survey evidence from 199 market associations in Lagos is consistent with the argument that politician threats (operationalized in this chapter as being in a market on local government land) motivate market leaders to promote trade in their markets. There is evidence that this relationship is stronger when traders sell different products and are thus less in competition with each other. The finding that better-governed markets are more likely to be politically engaged is consistent with a mechanism in which the leader needs the support of group members to mobilize against government threats.

My approach – asking respondents about group membership and group attributes, determining which respondents belong to the same group, and then examining the relationship between group attributes and theoretically important covariates – could be used in other contexts. For example, it could be used to better understand all sorts of informal associations, such as residential associations, and would be particularly useful when the universe of associations is unknown *ex ante*.

7

Private Groups in Comparative Perspective

Chapter 6 confirmed the finding from Chapter 5 that government threats are associated with better private governance. While Chapter 5 assessed government threats on a case-by-case basis, Chapter 6 focused on the vulnerability faced by markets located on local government land, an attribute that was straightforward to measure systematically across many market associations. Chapter 6 also showed that private governance is worse when traders are selling the same products. This is consistent with my theory that within-group competition will exacerbate collective action problems by, for example, increasing the costs to sharing information about trading partners with the market leader. The chapter also considered several factors that could shape trader cooperation, but this is distinct from good private governance. It is important to carefully theorize about how cooperation may shape group leader behavior, as I did in Chapter 4. For example, cooperation could facilitate market leader sanctioning. Lastly, the chapter showed that traders wishing to join a well-governed market association find it difficult to determine which ones these are before becoming a member.

The book makes two general contributions. First, it introduces a channel for economic development that does not rely on a benevolent government and strong respect for the rule of law. Second, it introduces a new factor to explain the persistence of private good governance. I discussed my expectations for the scope conditions of the argument in Chapter 4, proposing that it was particular to urban environments, where social embeddedness is less common and relational contracting harder to sustain. I also expected that the argument may not hold when the obstacles to sorting are lower, such as when there is greater transparency regarding which market associations are well governed.

In this chapter, I empirically assess the plausibility of these scope conditions and explore how my argument may apply to other types of groups in other contexts. I first briefly summarize the book and then assess the conditions under which government threats will motivate private good governance. Research on gang governance in Brazilian favelas shows that gang leaders provide services to residents (such as dispute resolution) in order to secure their loyalty and counter government pressure to turn on the gangs (Barnes, 2017). In the favelas, threats from private and state actors shape private governance in different ways. Likewise, evidence from street vendor associations in Mexico shows that the broad contours of my argument hold even when the hurdles to joining new associations are slightly lower. (Though if the obstacles to joining new groups were much lower, I suspect competition for group members would indeed increase the aggregate quality of private governance.) A market in Iran and a transportation association in Uganda put a finer point on the state threat variable, suggesting that, when the level of government meddling exceeds some threshold, it can fail to motivate better leader governance, and in some cases destroy the group. Evidence from associations in Ghanaian and Indian slums shows that social embeddedness is not sufficient for private good governance.

In the second half of the chapter I consider the policy implications of the book's findings. I propose that private governance – and, in turn, economic development – is best supported not by an absentee state or by massive state intervention in trade. Rather, a middle ground is ideal. I then argue that regardless of one's assumptions about how economic growth in private groups shapes the broader economy, since private groups control a massive portion of most economies, growth within these groups is important for its own sake.

7.1 SUMMARY OF BOOK

How do governments decide whether to use their strength to advance public or private interests? Several studies have explored this dilemma: a government that is strong enough to protect property rights and enforce contracts can also confiscate citizens' wealth (Weingast, 1995). To extend this research, this book considered this question in the context of *private* governance, looking at private groups and the private leaders who govern them. Private group leaders are able to provide services that support contractual trade. But with the power to enforce agreements comes the power to extort; indeed, many private leaders predate on their members. What explains group leader behavior? While much work focuses on determining why some organizations embrace state institutions to support trade and others rely on private institutions (e.g., Richman, 2017), my research examines places where state institutions do not support contractual trade, and works to explain variation in whether and how private leaders step up to the task.

Previous research on private governance focuses on groups that have sophisticated private pro-trade policies. Scholars focus on *describing* these private institutions and detailing *how* they promote trade (e.g., Stringham, 2015). While many such studies assume that trade-promoting private groups will emerge to fill gaps in the public provision of social order, such groups are rare in practice. Badly governed groups abound, but are often ignored.

The result has been the creation of a myth of spontaneous order, when in fact there are enormous hurdles to providing private institutions that establish order. In this book's primary case study, group leaders must be able to elicit information about dishonest traders, information which is hard to come by in competitive business environments when traders may benefit from other traders being cheated. Leaders must be willing to incur the social costs of ruling against their own traders when mediating disputes between group members and customers or suppliers based outside the market. Further, the power of group leaders must be checked in order to prevent them from extorting from their members. As Barak Richman notes, "sustaining [a] reputation mechanism demands a rigorous set of institutions. Reputation mechanisms do not arise easily and do not persist for long without institutional support" (2017, p. 61).

Many assume that group members' ability to avoid or leave groups curbs leader predation. If this were the case, it would force predatory leaders to change their behavior in order to keep their group intact. But I documented a series of obstacles to finding out about group conditions prior to joining, and another set of impediments – such as a limited number of optimal places to sell certain products – that make relocating difficult. The result is that traders stay in badly governed markets for quite a long time, and the mechanism of traders choosing to trade in better-governed markets is weak and thus does little to constrain extortion.

My results confirm those of previous studies which show that private groups can enable economic exchange in contexts where the public institutional environment does not protect property rights. Indeed, institutions in well-governed market associations in Lagos look remarkably similar to those in trading groups in medieval Europe (Greif, 2006) and contemporary prison gangs in America (Skarbek, 2014). But I have argued that the fact that group members would benefit from private pro-trade policies does not explain their existence. I have built on work by Elinor Ostrom (1990) and others to introduce an argument about the conditions under which group leaders will invest in pro-trade policies to promote trade. When the government keeps its hands off the economy, group leaders extort. Yet if the government threatens to intervene, leaders organize to resist for two reasons. First, a leader needs internal support in order to make credible threats to protest, which deters the leader from predating on group members. Second, a strong leader is motivated to police members' behavior to limit intervention from meddling public officials.

My argument is not about the state directly organizing the economy, nor do I maintain that the economy grows when the state stays out of market affairs. The argument, counterintuitively, is that, even when predatory politicians work against traders' interests, government officials unintentionally trigger private policies that benefit the traders. I advance a literature that has found support for this surprising path to growth in other places and times. Looking at how credit markets emerged in medieval England and colonial Uganda, Catherine Duggan found that "[i]ronically, the naissance of the formal credit sector was, largely, the result of the state's systematically disempowering lenders, rather than of powerful individuals making efforts to protect their capital" (Forthcoming). Minority groups were more vulnerable to the state than to the indigenous groups, and this was attractive to borrowers, who feared illegal collection from more socially powerful lenders. This led these minority groups

– Jews in medieval England and Asians in colonial Uganda – to develop a comparative advantage in lending. Duggan's narrative of political threats deterring opportunism echoes the argument presented in this book.

7.2 WHEN AND WHERE WILL STATE THREATS MOTIVATE STRONG LEADERS TO PROMOTE TRADE?

A wide range of groups have private leaders who can choose to act either in or against the interests of group members. In this section I discuss the extent to which my theory can shed light on internal dynamics in other associations, as well as its limits. I look primarily at urban associations, assessing private governance in Brazilian gangs, Mexican street vendor associations, a market in Tehran, a Ugandan transport association, neighborhood associations in urban Ghana and India, and a global chemical manufacturer association.

Criminal Governance in Brazil's Favelas
Gang governance in Rio de Janeiro illustrates how government threats can generate good private governance outside of Lagos. Nicholas Barnes writes about gangs that control territory within a favela to direct a local drug trade (Barnes, 2017). He argues that Rio's Military Police motivate gangs to provide services to residents – including dispute resolution and preventing loud music from playing at night – to gain their support for two reasons. The first is to reduce the likelihood that conflicts will escalate to involve the police. The second reason is to prevent residents from supplying information about gang members to the Military Police. This is persuasive evidence that my theory's two mechanisms extend beyond Lagos: the group leader (1) keeps their house in order to keep the state out and (2) builds member support to limit state intrusion.

This case also suggests that state and non-state threats have different impacts on private governance. Barnes shows that the prospect of territorial intrusion by rival gangs (i.e., a non-state threat) makes gangs *more* predatory and coercive. With territorial disputes the gang is confronting the rival gang directly and will engage in more acts of violence – including against non-gang members – to ensure its rules are followed, especially around the border area. Intergang competition, then, does not result in better private governance. More broadly, this suggests that inter-associational competition may lack the productive impetus of state threats.

Street Vendor Governance in Mexico City
Mexico City street vendor associations are another example of predatory leadership – in particular predatory and preferential leadership – in private groups. John Cross writes about how local officials give certain street vendor associations permission to govern the vending in a particular area (1998). If a street vendor seeks a semi-legitimate "tolerated" status, the vendor must belong to an association, which ranges in size from being relatively small to having 10,000

members. In one such association, a leader accused by members of fraud ultimately served prison time (1998). In another case, a leader assigned stalls based on perceptions of vendor loyalty.

Frictions to sorting can sustain these associations. Though street vendors do not have shops, which can reduce the hurdles of relocating to a new vending area with a new association if their current one becomes too predatory, there are still substantial costs to moving. The semi-illegal nature of street vending increases the costs of sorting into new trading areas, as vendors rely on associations for permission to trade. Additionally, if a vendor moves, they will lose their clientele (1998, p. 157).

These obstacles make it easier for leaders to use authoritarian tactics and predate, but vendors' ability to relocate means that leaders cannot exercise absolute power. Leaders aim to increase the area and number of vendors they control, but only if they can continue to advocate for an increasingly bigger group, as vendors will leave if they do not feel protected – the primary purpose the association serves for them. To secure government protection, leaders must be able to mobilize vendors to protest or rally. The prospect of "shock troops" can help associations make demands on politicians, in particular demands to continue trading in an area. But to survive, leaders "must provide a competitive 'package' of benefits and costs for their members," Cross writes. "[T]he most important weapon vendors have is simply to leave a leader who fails to protect prime commercial areas or who charges too much in fees and political activism" (1998, pp. 156–157). This dynamic is remarkably similar to what I describe in Lagos markets, where if leaders want to mobilize traders to make demands on politicians, they must operate in a way that allows them to amass such support.

In short, leaders must strike a delicate balance. If they aim to increase their rents, which derive from vendor fees, they could both predate and compel vendors to protest and rally frequently by threatening to rescind their right to trade. In the short term this might increase their rents. But such a scenario will not be sustainable, as over the long term vendors will leave. For this reason, badly governed street vendor associations may not last as long as the badly governed market associations in Lagos. But these associations face similar incentives and constraints, and the evidence suggests leaders may be motivated to govern well to increase their long-term goal of collecting rents and providing political protection.

Private Governance in the Tehran Bazaar

Arang Keshavarzian writes about historical variation in self-governance in Iran's Tehran Bazaar, a market with about 40,000 shops (2007). According to Keshavarzian, under Mohammad Reza Pahlavi, the shah from 1941 to 1979, self-governance in the bazaar thrived. After the Islamic Revolution, things fell apart in the bazaar.

The shah had grand modernizing ambitions and did not believe the bazaar was aligned with those goals. He publicly railed against the bazaaris, describing them as "a fistful of beaded bazaar idiots" (Mozaffari, 1991). He set up parallel Western-style retail markets that threatened the traders' businesses. Consistent with my argument, social cohesion and reputational trade thrived during this period.

The shah's threats led to "a very strong 'ingroup feeling'" and "the antibazaar sentiment that prevailed among the political and intellectual elite generated a defensive banding together by the bazaaris" (Keshavarzian, 2007). Good private governance in the bazaar was partly motivated by a desire to keep the state out. The shah's secret police struggled to monitor the bazaar, as the traders were quick to independently identify suspicious individuals and behavior (Ghandchi-Tehrani, 1983). This cohesiveness made the bazaar politically powerful. It closed fifty times – sometimes for up to three days – to protest the shah's policies (Keshavarzian, 2007, p. 237). When the bazaaris faced threats, their social cohesion allowed them to mobilize due to a "common fate with respect to market conditions" (Parsa, 1989). In short, state threats incentivized good private governance.

Why did reputational trade thrive in this period? The main associations were religious gatherings, where in addition to religious rituals, members pooled funds to support traders who were struggling and "sanctioned bazaaris who broke 'the rules' by spreading rumors about them" (p. 94). There were also ethnic-based associations and weekly meetings for women. Keshavarzian argues that these meetings were spaces for people to organically share information about other traders.

Trade brokers also played an important role in sustaining reputational incentives. By connecting wholesalers and retailers, they had a wealth of information about the behavior of many traders. This is not the case in Lagos markets, where brokers play only a marginal role since traders typically find suppliers independently; traders often report finding wholesalers by shopping the "open market." Variation in the use of brokers could be a productive area for future research.

Meanwhile, after the Islamic Revolution, Islamic leaders saw themselves as allied with the bazaar. But government policies conspired to destroy the bazaar's strong reputational mechanisms. The leader of the Islamic Association of China and Glassware Guild of Tehran said these policies – such as government efforts to co-opt traders with larger businesses by appointing them to government posts – divided traders and resulted in a drop in association meeting attendance. The Islamic regime's actions ruptured the bazaar's cohesion. At the same time, Iran experienced an economic crisis caused by international sanctions, the invasion by Iraq, and the government's nationalization of important sectors like banking and shipping. Many bazaaris left Iran, and the bazaar saw new entrants, which reduced trust. The Islamic regime also closed down many of the places where traders had gathered socially, like public baths and large restaurants, which reduced their social cohesion. And the regime mandated that one of the bazaar's associations monitor traders to ensure they followed state regulations and prices, which further reduced trust. When Keshavarzian asked a bazaari for the name of a guild leader, the trader asked why he wanted to talk to an Islamic association: "Why do you want to interview these people? Nobody takes them seriously anymore. They just parrot what the government says and never do anything for us" (p. 162).

While some level of state threat may lead to better private governance, the post-revolution bazaar shows that too much state intrusion can be disastrous. The Islamic leaders did not just threaten the market; they radically restructured it (Keshavarzian, 2007, p. 10). By weakening the market's cohesion, the market became politically weaker as well. In 2001 carpet sellers tried to organize a strike to protest the lack of police investigation into a spate of burglaries, but many refused to close their shops for the strike.

The bazaar's history illuminates a phenomenon I was not able to observe in Lagos markets: a shift in private governance equilibria. The Islamic Revolution transformed the nature of state threats against the bazaar, from being just serious enough to motivate internal cooperation to being so intense that it was not possible to fight back. This resulted in a form of collusion, with the co-optation of influential traders. Future work could theorize about the causes of these equilibrium shifts.

The Uganda Taxi Operators and Drivers Association

At its peak, the Uganda Taxi Operators and Drivers Association (UTODA) had roughly 100,000 members, including drivers and vehicle owners (Goodfellow, 2016). It had a national chairman, along with district-level positions, including district chairmen, vice-chairmen, and executive secretaries (Goodfellow, 2016). UTODA is an example of a predatory association with exclusive institutions. It illustrates how predatory groups can hold on for decades, but ultimately its inability to gain the sympathies of its members made the group politically weak and led to its downfall.

Though UTODA members included both vehicle owners and drivers, only owners could hold executive roles. Drivers were relegated to lower-level positions, like welfare officers, and felt that the association extorted from them. In addition to the monthly price for a sticker that allowed them to operate, they paid unreceipted welfare and loading fees. While UTODA remitted some funds to the Kampala City Council, the association's leaders pocketed roughly 90 percent of their $24 million annual income (Goodfellow, 2016).

In 2010 the legislature replaced the Kampala City Council with the Kampala City Council Authority. The Ugandan president was able to exert more control over the new authority, including by appointing its directors. The head of the authority viewed UTODA as a threat, and imported buses which were in direct competition with UTODA. The authority demanded that UTODA members pay fees directly to the authority, as opposed to through the association. In response to frustration about UTODA's unreceipted fee collections, a faction within the association announced a new organization, the Drivers and Conductors Central Association (Goodfellow, 2016 citing Nalugo and Kostov, 2011). The City Council Authority also challenged UTODA's contract to manage the city's taxi park. UTODA brought the authority to court; after a year of litigation, UTODA lost.

In essence, the government destroyed UTODA. While it is impossible to say for sure, if UTODA had better represented the interests of its 100,000 members, it might not have had the breakaway group and might have been able to mobilize its members to fight back against the new Kampala City Council Authority policies, and perhaps win the court case. Even in an authoritarian regime, the prospect of protest by such a large group of people can shape policy.

This narrative raises two questions. First, why did UTODA continue extorting in the face of threats? Threats from the former Kampala City Council had been weak, but those from the Kampala City Council Authority became more extreme, and UTODA may not have had enough time to adjust. Second, why did UTODA members fail to mobilize against their leadership for so long? Goodfellow suspects this is because most drivers – who were excluded from UTODA leadership – imagined that one day they would be bus owners, and then represented by the group (2016). In short, the case of UTODA shows that in the absence of serious government threats group leaders can extort, that a predatory association can persist for decades, and that sorting into better managed groups is not straightforward.

Associations in Poor Neighborhoods in Ghana and India

Slums around the world are governed by associations. In India, for example, informal associational leadership is almost as common as in Lagos markets. In a survey across eighty slums, 77 percent of residents reported informal leadership in their neighborhood (Auerbach, 2016). Just as markets face threats of demolition from politicians working to modernize communities, slums face threats of demolition, and slum leaders similarly try to mobilize residents to fend off demolition (Paller, 2019).

Jeffrey Paller argues that association leaders in Ghanaian slums lose residents' respect and support if they do not act in their interests (2019, p. 126). "Leaders must contribute to the public good to legitimate their authority" (p. 139). This in turn "provides them with the political capital to get things done" (p. 139). When slum leaders have the support of residents, they can bargain with politicians, offering the prospect of their residents' political support in the future. They can also grant politician requests for youth residents to patrol polling stations and attend rallies. In 2009, for example, more than 20,000 Old Fadama residents stayed home from work and attended a large demonstration against an eviction threat. At 4:00 AM, community leaders stopped residents from going to work. By 10:00 AM, thousands of people were on the streets (p. 196). Following this demonstration, the government announced that it would investigate relocating – rather than evicting – residents.

While slum leaders may use their political might to demand services for their community – such as to help residents obtain government documents, or services like road paving, or fighting eviction threats – they can also make demands to benefit themselves, for example, requesting government jobs, as Adam Auerbach notes happens in India (Auerbach, 2017).

Slum leaders are distinct from market leaders in three ways that might make them more representative. First, residential group leaders will be more embedded in the daily lives of group members, given that they live in the same area, which could constrain extortion. Second, at least in the Indian context, residents have some choice over which leader they choose to be under, which might lead leaders to compete over better governance (Auerbach and Thachil, 2018). Third, slum leaders often aspire to be politicians, which is not as common in Lagos markets, perhaps because slums often contain more members than market associations. In other ways, however, one can imagine representativeness not being assumed. As in the Lagos markets, slum leaders can have outside business interests that might give them different incentives from those of their residents. In India, 7 percent of slum leaders had government jobs, 4 percent were lawyers, doctors, accountants, or engineers, 2 percent were educators, and 14 percent had businesses outside the slum, like mechanics, barbers, or retail stores (Auerbach, 2017).

In short, while slum leaders may be more vulnerable to constraints on their power than market leaders, this does not guarantee that they will represent their residents' interests. Further, accounts from Ghana and India suggest that private associations can perceive a government's modernizing ambitions as a threat; as in Lagos, leaders must represent member interests in order to politically mobilize residents to fend off these threats.

The Chemical Manufacturing Industry

The chemical manufacturing industry's attempts at internal regulation demonstrate that the hurdles to self-governance theorized in this book are not unique to developing countries. In 1984 lax management at an Indian pesticide plant resulted in the Bhopal disaster, a gas leak that killed thousands. Chemical manufacturers quickly realized they faced a reputational collective action problem: since residents did not distinguish between them, all of their reputations were at risk (Nash and Ehrenfeld, 1997). The following year, Responsible Care was created, a global agreement that encouraged members to meet (vague) goals like making the environment a priority. Though signatories such as the American Chemical Manufacturers' Association (CMA) had the power to create more stringent codes for its members, it did not do so. The CMA created management practice codes that were similarly vague and hard to assess compliance with. Though Responsible Care allows member trade associations (such as the CMA) to revoke the membership of firms that do not comply, as of 1997 the CMA had never done this. The CMA had a third-party verification system to assess firm management systems, but consenting to third-party verification was only recommended, not mandatory (Nash and Ehrenfeld, 1997).

Not surprisingly, opportunism persisted after the creation of Responsible Care (King and Lenox, 2000). Signatories of the agreement were no more likely to improve their environmental practices than non-signatories. Though leaders had the power to sanction opportunism, they also had the power to sanction in order to pursue private interests: "Industry members may fear that powerful association members may use sanctions strategically to punish weaker members and limit overall competition" (King and Lenox, 2000, p. 713).

It is tempting to conclude that chemical manufacturing private governance has been ineffective because its institutions lacked teeth. But that is not really an explanation. The CMA, for example, could have created codes that had teeth, but did not. *Why* they did not is an important question that should be explained. Indeed, research on the CMA's internal compliance schemes makes points that mirror the one made in this book: successful compliance schemes are often developed as a strategy to avoid lawsuits. But in short, the history of the CMA shows that the ability of group leaders to invest in and implement costly trade-promoting policies cannot be assumed, and that the fear of private leader predation exists in the West as well.

7.2.1 Cities in Weak Democracies

The most precise way to describe the bounds of the argument is to say that it applies (1) in contexts without social embeddedness (most likely cities) and (2) where the rule of law is weak but not absent (typically weak democracies). In cities, rapid population growth can make communities more ethnically, linguistically, and economically diverse – what Auerbach et al. term greater social diversity (2018). In more homogenous communities, group cooperation is easier to sustain because social pressure makes secretive and dishonest behavior less common. In these areas, private group leaders will be less critical, or at least their jobs will be easier as it should be easier to elicit valuable information from traders. Second, when laws are impartially and efficiently enforced, private associations are less important. The activities they might undertake – impartial dispute resolution, for example – are less needed, as a neutral legal system backstops individual cooperation. Yet in the absence of even a partially formed legal system, state threats will be disorganized – which is unlikely to motivate better private governance.

Further, the case of the Tehran Bazaar suggests that my argument might not apply in very repressive authoritarian regimes, where even the strongest private associations may be unable to threaten politicians. Since electoral incentives will be weaker, the prospect of a market association protesting may be irrelevant. Politicians in these regimes would also be more likely to impose leaders on groups, which would curtail a leader's ability to mobilize group members.

Even strong market leaders will struggle to fend off government threats when group members are politically disempowered – for example, when group members are immigrants. In Equatorial Guinea – which has one of the most repressive regimes in the world – I once visited a market in the capital city comprised primarily of Nigerian traders. These traders did everything possible to avoid encounters with the police or other state officials who would harass them regardless of whether their immigration documents were in order. It is virtually impossible to imagine traders in this market trying to threaten any public official.

Finally, my argument will have less explanatory power for groups if members can more easily switch groups. It is not clear if there are many groups like this – particularly those that relate to trade. There were substantial barriers to group switching in all of the group examples discussed earlier. But if individual members could (1) easily change groups and (2) acquire reliable information about governance in the relevant universe of groups, this could theoretically constrain leader predation.

Could the balance of politically powerful groups and politician threats instead generate compromise and mutually beneficial outcomes? An adversarial relationship can and often does lead to collaboration, where cooperation is sustained by the implicit possibility of undiscussed threats. This book has focused on how power balances generate private good governance, but it can lead to other positive outcomes as well. For example, there is a politically powerful market in the north of Lagos that is under the jurisdiction of a proactive local government. Several years ago this local government wanted to renovate the market, and as usual the market did not want that to happen. In this instance, the market and local government reached a remarkable compromise: the market would cooperate with the renovation, but part of the new market would be reserved for – and financially accessible to – the original traders. The market is now a one-story plaza in front, where new traders sell expensive items like refrigerators. Behind, there is a clean and orderly large outdoor area with a cement floor and a tin roof. The original traders sell produce and meat from this area and feel satisfied with the arrangement. I suspect mutual threats can lead to positive outcomes like this one in many contexts.

7.3 BROADER IMPLICATIONS

Many believe the state should keep its hands off the economy, especially where the rule of law is weak, due to the expectation that private governance will emerge if needed. This view can lead to detrimental policies. My findings suggest that, in the absence of the threat of state interference, private leaders may extort. Exchanges with public officials motivate market leaders to invest in costly trade-promoting policies like information sharing. Ineffective public officials may therefore be effective in a generative way.

But a predatory government is not a necessary condition for the argument. Indeed, I am agnostic as to whether the types of actions governments take that markets perceive to be threatening are "bad." For example, market renovations can improve sanitation, and perhaps support commercial activity in general. And simply because a market perceives a raise in local government fees as unfair does not necessarily mean they are a bad idea – perhaps the local government plans to use the funds to improve a local road. The point is simply that group leaders can respond productively to government actions that they *perceive* to be undesirable.

The finding that competition impedes good private governance is important, as the gains from pro-trade policies are higher when traders are selling the same product. A fabric seller would certainly appreciate information – which may have come from an electronics seller – about market customers who are known to buy on credit and not repay. But information from another fabric trader about the trustworthiness of fabric suppliers would be more useful; being defrauded in a wholesale purchase is more costly than a customer failing to balance their debt from a single transaction. Cooperation with traders dealing in the same product could also deter future suppliers from cheating them. This would work if the traders signaled to suppliers that they were cooperating and were prepared to boycott any supplier who cheated a member of their network. A similar logic holds for customers, but the potential gains are greater for the larger transactions with suppliers.

Elinor Ostrom has observed that, when one assumes all common pool resources are vulnerable to the tragedy of the commons, too often one concludes that the only policy option is the privatization of property at one extreme, or government ownership at the other (2005). Ostrom's canonical research on communities solving collective action problems on their own of course disputes the notion that privatization and public ownership are the only policy solutions (1990). Similarly, I do not want to propose that the state should impose leaders on private groups. But the notion that an absentee state promotes private good governance is misguided. Working within the structures of an organized state might be preferable – even if the state is predatory.

Three policy implications follow from the finding that within-group competition both mediates the relationship between politician threats and private good governance, and generally has a negative association with private good governance. First, while this book has focused on associations that represent traders in a specific location, groups that connect traders selling the same product in different parts of a city would be fruitful. For example, a network of fabric sellers in which no member competes with another is possible to imagine. Members could share information about suppliers without the fear it will affect their own business. While such a group could overcome the competition barrier and help traders avoid "bad types," there are limits to the value of such a group. In particular, because these groups would necessarily be small, they may not enjoy a deterrent effect. A boycott of just ten traders is unlikely to scare a supplier. Peter Leeson would call this "less encompassing multilateral punishment" (2014).

The second policy implication pertains to group leaders. Eliciting information about fraudsters is a collective action problem: everyone would reap the benefits of having this information, but they will be tempted to withhold their own valuable information to prevent a competitor from gaining an edge. Knowing this, market associations could work to convert information from a club good (i.e., a local public good provided to everyone in the association) to a good that leaders offer or withhold conditional on a member's contribution. This is how credit unions work: banks cannot receive information about new customer creditworthiness without sharing information with other banks about the creditworthiness of their existing customers. Similarly, the website Glassdoor.com limits the amount of information a user can see about the salaries of employees at other companies until they have shared information about their own job.

Third, group leaders could underscore the benefits of multilateral punishment strategies available to a trader only if they share information. Returning to the credit union example, banks benefit from customers knowing that they will share their behavior with other banks. A customer is less likely to default on a loan if they know that information will be shared with other potential loan providers. Banks decide whether to join credit unions by weighing the deterrent effects with the competitive effects (Padilla and Pagano, 1997). Interventions that alter such a trade-off for traders could lead to large gains.

7.4 PRIVATE GOVERNANCE AND GROUP MEMBER BUSINESS OUTCOMES

What are the implications of private governance for trade? I expected better private governance to be associated with better business outcomes, but the data do not support this prediction. There is no relationship between market leader governance and a number of outcomes related to the size of a trader's business – the number of employees, the value of their stock, the total cost of goods purchased in the previous year, whether the trader imports directly, and whether the trader sells mostly wholesale.[1] Why might this be?

One path that should connect better market governance to improved trade outcomes is that customers know that certain markets are less likely to have traders who will cheat them. Customers would therefore shop in better-governed markets. However, customers might have only a vague sense of how useful and fair leaders of different markets would be if a dispute occurred. They may also shop at a particular market out of habit or due to its convenient location, and might thus be unlikely to shop at a different market even if the quality of goods available there was more reliable.

An additional possibility is that these trade outcomes are only distally related to market governance. Perhaps if the survey had asked about more proximate trade outcomes, such as how often customers buy on credit and fail to repay, I would have observed a relationship. Still, I caution against interpreting the lack of a relationship between good private governance and business outcomes as a true null finding, because it is difficult to elicit truthful information from traders about their revenue. In any event, the relationship between private governance and trade outcomes is an exciting area for further research. Future work could even compare product quality across markets.

7.5 SHIFTING EQUILIBRIA

Much of this book has discussed the frictions that keep associations stuck in an equilibrium. For example, I have argued that a shift in the products traders sell could theoretically increase or decrease competition, which could in turn shape private governance. But traders do not switch products frequently. Still, changes in private governance are not impossible to imagine.

---

[1] See Appendix E.

A drop in group social cohesion that weakens traders' ability to constrain a leader's behavior is plausible. For instance, this could happen if a local government renovated a market and displaced traders. When the new market reopened, most traders would be new and not know each other. Similarly, the government could destroy an informal residential settlement, with only some original inhabitants returning. These changes can be pernicious for private governance; besides the destruction of any prior cohesion, the original group leader may keep their position and feel little obligation to new members.

Changes in government strength – for example, through regime transitions – could also cause equilibria shifts. First, if politicians gained power vis-à-vis a group and dramatically stepped up group interference, this could destroy private good governance. This is what happened in the Tehran Bazaar, as described earlier. Beyond a certain threshold, government intrusion will not motivate leaders to support trade, but will instead cause division and disorder. Second, an increase in political instability – through a coup or violent conflict – would leave private groups without an organized state entity with which to negotiate. If it is the interchange between public officials and a group leader that shapes leader behavior, when there is no entity to negotiate with, a group leader may extort. Alternatively, a new organized threat could emerge. In theory this could alter market leader behavior for the better. But this may not work in the short term. Leaders can be set in their ways, and it takes time to internalize and act on new incentives.

Additionally, three changes that enable relational contracting could obviate the need for some services that well-governed associations offer. First, larger firms would not need to be part of a group that could boycott in order to deter cheating: the threat of losing business with their own firm would be sufficient. One reason private governance is so important is because of the failure of relational contracting in many places. As discussed in Chapter 4, relational contracting can fail when the prospect of a large supplier losing business from a single small trader is not much to fear. Where there is uncertainty about whether a supplier acted maliciously or made an innocent mistake, or whether someone else along the supply chain is at fault, suppliers may rationally cheat. It takes a coalition of traders to deter supplier opportunism. When a buyer is bigger, however, the threat to a supplier of losing its business changes this calculus. For instance, it is hard to imagine a Chinese supplier cheating Walmart. The implication is that, as firms in developing countries grow, private associations may be less critical.

Why developing country firms are small is the topic of a large literature in economics. One finding from big experimental studies is that access to capital is a barrier to growth (De Mel, McKenzie and Woodruff, 2008; McKenzie and Woodruff, 2008). Firms could grow as banking systems develop and learn to assess the creditworthiness of unconventional credit applicants and profitably supply smaller loans. Several start-ups are working to bring credit to people who are unbanked or lack a credit history. Juvo, for example, works with mobile operators in Latin America, Southeast Asia, and Eastern Europe to give users increasingly larger amounts of phone credit on credit, helping unbanked individuals develop a credit profile so that Juvo can provide larger

loans to them. Two companies, Branch and Tala, assess an individual's creditworthiness with data from their smartphone usage and provide loans within
minutes. Creditinfo assesses loan applicants with a personality quiz.

Firm expansion through vertical integration – when two firms that control
different stages of a supply chain merge – could also diminish the importance
of associations. Vertical integration can be useful when transaction costs are
large (Williamson, 1971), like when relational contracting fails. When a firm
becomes both the seller and the buyer, services like information sharing about
suppliers are unnecessary.

The second change is that a more developed wholesale distribution network
could support relational contracting by reducing the number of middlemen in
a transaction. With fewer middlemen, buyers could more easily assess who in
a supply chain is at fault for damaged goods. Third, political and currency sta-
bility could also enable relational contracting by lengthening trading partners'
time horizons, which reduces the temptation to cheat. In short, these are three
types of economic shifts that would make relational contracting more likely to
succeed and make private governance less important.

7.6 PRIVATE GOVERNANCE AND THE ECONOMY

Moving beyond the market, how does private group order shape the broader
economy? There are reasons to be pessimistic about the externalities of group
order. Some research on medieval guilds suggests that guilds not only did *not*
benefit non-group members, but that they impeded general economic growth
by buying privileges from political elites that made the playing field uneven
(Ogilvie, 2014). But in the absence of a strong rule of law, it is not clear that
generalized economic growth is the appropriate counterfactual (North, Wallis
and Weingast, 2009). Further, there are many beneficiaries of group order. In
developing countries about 41 percent of GDP comes from the informal sector
(Schneider, 2005), and the associational structure of informal trade is a global
phenomenon (e.g., Cross, 1998). Future research on the externalities of group
order should consider questions such as whether a group lobbies for excludable
club goods or public goods, and whether the outcome of interest is economic
growth or *equitable* economic growth.

Alison Post has observed that "low-income urban voters often approach
the state through intermediaries or brokers" (2018, p. 10). For many, market
associations are the primary intermediary, and the importance of the informal
sector is not expected to diminish anytime soon. Prior studies suggest that
informal trade thrives with globalization (Milner and Rudra, 2015). But there
have been few large comparative studies of these groups. My research has shed
light on the inner workings of modern informal economies and introduced the
conditions under which pro-growth policies are observed in associations that
govern informal trade, which account for a vast amount of global economic
output.

Appendix A

Appendix to Chapter 2 – Market Associations: An Overview

A.1 ORGANIZATION OF INFORMAL TRADE IN LAGOS

This book focused on a particular type of informal association, namely market associations, the main association for traders in this context. Figure A.1 shows the broader organization of informal trade in Lagos, and which level of government associations liaise with. Commodity unions, for example, are associations for traders selling particular products. The main purpose of commodity unions is price fixing, but the effectiveness of the price fixing is highly variable. Not all of these associations exist everywhere, and many are extremely weak.

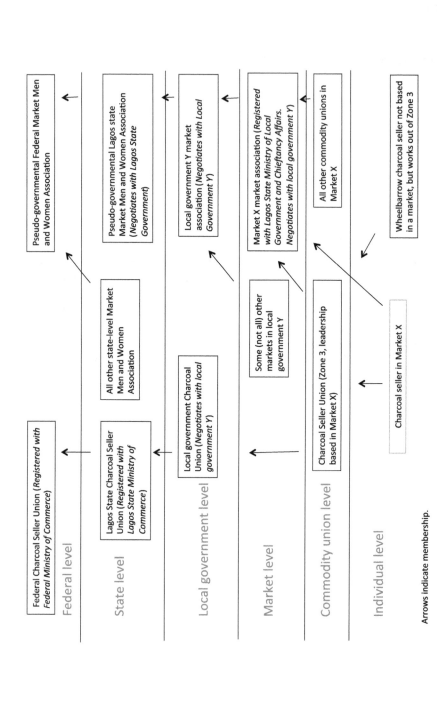

FIGURE A.1 The organization of informal trade in Lagos

Appendix B

Appendix to Chapter 3 – Conducting a Representative Survey of Informal Traders

B.1 LIST OF MARKET ASSOCIATIONS IN THE SURVEY

This is a list of associations represented in the 2015 trader survey.

15A Oremeji Street Plaza Association & 19 Opebi Road Association
34 Egbeda Shop Owner Association & 34 Plaza Market Association
5 Oshitelu Street Complex Association & 5 Otigba Street Plaza Association
6 Ola Ayeni Street & 7 Idowu Lane Shopping Complex
8 Idowu Lane Plaza Association & 8 Ola Ayeni Street Plaza Association
AB Plaza Association & Abeni Plaza Association
Abia Plaza Association & Abuja Plaza Association
Ajao Plaza Association & Alaba Traders Association
Alakoro Market Association & Alasho Association
Allied Shopping Plaza Association & Amalgamated
Amalgamated Association & Ampanda Phone Accessories Association
  (Oroyinyin Area)
Anamabra Traders Association & Anikantamo Plank Market Association
AO Trader Association & Associated Footwear and Allied Product
Association of Cosmetic and Hair Product & Association of Progressive Traders
Association of Ready-Made Clothing & Association of Salon and Hairstyles
Association of Weave-On Traders/Kawa Union & Atunrase Market Association
Audio Video Sellers Association of Nigeria & Auto Spare Parts and Machinery
  Dealers Association
Bakky Plaza Association & Balogun Bags (Hang Bags) Association
Balogun Business Association & Balogun Childrens Wears Association
Balogun Ladies Dress Association & Balogun Shoe Association
Balogun Traders Association & Bauchi Cluster Association
Bauchi Shoe and Sandal Association & Bayelsa Association
Benue Plaza Association & Block B11A Plaza Association
Bolashodun Plaza Association & Borno Cluster Association
Breadfruit Traders Association & C&S Plaza Association
C11 Plaza Traders Association & Carlous Plaza Association
CD Marketers/Producers Association & Cherub Mall Association

Christian Association & Computer and Allied Products Dealers Association of Nigeria

Corner Stone Block B Association & De-Line Market Association

Delta Plaza Cluster Association & Designer Plaza Union in Gbajumo

Destiny Plaza Traders Association & Diamond Plaza Association

Doherty Traders Association & Dosunmo - Estate of Adeniyi Brothers Landlord Association

Dosunmo Ebun Eko Book Sellers Association & Dosunmo, Alhaji Rufai Ajala House

Dosunmo/Obun Eko Market Association & Ebonyi Plaza Association

Ebute Ero Market Community Association & Ekiti Plaza Cluster Association

Eko Plaza Association & Electrical Dealers Association

Electro-Textile Market Association & Emab Union Association

Enugu Youth Association & Ereko Balogun Market Association

Euro-Asia Plaza Association & F Line Traders Association

Fajol Complex Committee & Fancy Furniture Dealers Association

Fancy Traders Association & Fashion and Tailoring Materials Association

Fashion Designer Association/Balogun Fashion Wear Association & Finished Textiles Association

Francine Dealer Association & G Line Section Association

Gateway Market Association & Gbajumo Market Association

Gbajumo Shoe Trader Union & GBO Market Association

George and Lace Dealers Association & Gift Marketing Alliance

God is Able Plaza Association & God's Favour Plaza

Good Hope & Great Nigeria Plaza Traders Association

GSM Plaza Association (Lagos Island) & GSM Plaza Association (Victoria Island)

GTB Plaza Association & H Line Association

H Plaza Landlord Association & Haggai Plaza Association

HAWAN & Ibukunoluwa Lace Association

Idera Market Association & Idowu Lane Association

Ifelodun Bristol Traders/Market Association & Ifelodun Market Association

Ifelodun Phone Accessories Association & Igbehin-Adun Market Association

Igbo Union Association & Igbo Union Association (Oniru)

Ijaiye Gutter Lace Association & Ikota Shopping Complex Association

Imo Plaza Association & Importers Association of Nigeria

Industrial Market Association & International Market Association Electronics Sector

International Market Electrical Association (IMEA) & Iron Dealers Association

Ise Oluwa Plaza Market Association & Italian Set Association, Balogun Market

Iya Loga Onigele & Kaduna Traders Association

Kano Market Plaza & Katsina Plaza Clusters

Kebbi Plaza 1 Association & Kitchen Utensil Association

KK Ventures & Kogi Cluster Association

Lacasadbils & Lagoon Plaza Association

Lagoon Plaza Women Association & Lagos Plaza Committee of Traders

Leather Association & MA Dallas United Federal Association

Maja Plaza Association & Mandelas United Traders Association

Niger 1 2 3 4 Cluster Association & Niger 2 Plaza Association

Oba Elegushi Market Association & Obadina Plaza Association

Oja Oba Plaza Association & Oja Oba Provision Association

Ojo International Traders Centre & Ojomu Royal Market Association

Oke Arin Market Association & Oko Awo Market Association

Olojo Drive Association & Oluwole Union Shopping Mall Association

One Love Association & Oniru Market Association
Oniru Market Provisions/Toiletries Association & Opticians Association
Oroyinyin Traders Association & Otigba Association
Owolewa Plaza Association & Owolowo Textile Market Association
Oyo Cluster Meeting & Paul and Mike Association
Peace Plaza Association & Phone Accessories Association
Phone Dealer Association & Phone Union Association
Plastic Dealers Association & Plateau Cluster Association
Powa Plaza Phase 1 Association & Powa Plaza Phase 3 Association
Prince Plaza Traders Committee & Progress Plaza Association
Progressive Auto and Article Dealers Association & Qubest Plaza Union
Queen's Plaza Association & Radio Nigeria Plaza Association
Rivers Cluster Association & Saliu Aliu Market Association
Samuis Plaza Landlord/Caretaker Association & Sangotedo Traders Association
Scapular Plaza Association & Sebuff Plaza Association
Shoe and Bag Association & Sokoto Plaza Association
St. Peter Ibidoja Association & Stationary Dealers Association
Sura Shopping Plaza Association & Taiwo Plaza Association
Technical Association & Topaz Plaza Association
Turkish Product Finished Dealer Association & Union Home Association
United Island Business Association & United Trader Association
Unity Plaza Association & Victory Plaza Association
White House Association & Wine and Beverages Association
Wowo Oni Pala Association & Ziba Shoe Plaza Association
Zone B17 Plaza Association

Appendix C

Appendix to Chapter 4 – A Calm Sea Does not Make a Good Sailor: A Theory of Private Good Governance

C.1 RELATIONAL CONTRACTING

TABLE C.1 *Frequency of defective products, by length of relationship, in years, between supplier and buyer. Models 2 and 3 control for the total cost of the purchase.*

	Dependent variable		
	Products have defects		
	(1)	(2)	(3)
Length of relationship with suppliers	−0.001**	−0.002*	−0.001
	(0.001)	(0.001)	(0.002)
Constant	0.047***	0.043***	0.004
	(0.005)	(0.005)	(0.035)
Controls	No	Yes	Yes
Trader fixed effects	No	No	Yes
Observations	3,627	2,866	2,866
R^2	0.001	0.001	0.378

Note: *p<0.1; **p<0.05; ***p<0.01

Appendix D

Appendix to Chapter 6 – Government Threats and Within-Group Competition

D.1 SURVEY QUESTIONS

Variable	Survey question
Explanatory variables	
Land	Is this plaza/market on private land or local government land, or some other type of land? Variable construction: I use the modal response to this question among traders in a given association.
Product diversification	What type of products does this business sell? Variable construction: From a list thirteen product options, I group these into five broader categories. I then create an index that sums the squares of the proportion of traders selling in these product categories, and subtract that value from one.
Outcome variables	
Representativeness	Do the association executives represent your interests?
Private extortion	Do the association executives account properly for the fees they collect?
Free to complain	Do traders here feel free to complain to the executives?
Help resolve disputes	Have the association executives helped you resolve any dispute with other traders here in the past one year?
Controls, mechanisms, and alternative explanatory factors	
Trader education	What is the highest level of education that you have completed? Variable construction: This variable takes one if the trader has any post secondary education, and zero otherwise.
Number of employees	How many paid employees does this business currently have? Do not include yourself, or any apprentices, unpaid or casual workers.
Annual rent	How much do you pay to use your shop and any stores or warehouse space?
Product sold	What type of products does this business sell? Variable construction: From a list thirteen product options, I group these into five broader categories.
Leader tenure	Does the leader hold their position for life?
Market leader political power	Do the association executives here provide information about politicians prior to elections? Has someone ever asked traders in this association to sleep in their shops before voting day?
Length of time in market	What year did you begin trading in this particular plaza?
Ethnic diversity	To which ethnic group do you belong? Variable construction: I create an index that sums the squares of the proportion of traders in each ethnic group, and subtract that value from one.
Local government of residence	What local government do you reside in currently?
Reason for choosing market	What attracted you to this plaza? (pilot only) Variable construction: This was an open response question that was then coded.
Total stock value	What is the approximate value in total of all products you currently have in stock? Please remember that we will keep your personal information strictly confidential.
Market association size	Please, can you estimate, how many traders belong to [assocname]? (This question was asked in the second round of this panel survey in 2016.) Variable construction: I take the average response to this question among traders in a given association.

FIGURE D.1 Survey questions used in the paper

D.2 NOTE ON LAND TYPE

To determine the type of land a market association is on, I use the modal response to the question "Is this market on private land or local government land, or some other type of land?" One commercial area, which encompasses several market associations in the sample, is on federal government land. The founding traders leased this land specifically because they believed the federal government would be a relatively absentee landlord (interview with local government official on April 25, 2013). Because the circumstances surrounding this commercial area are so unique, I exclude its traders from the main analysis (which is why the N in the main tables does not equal 1,179).

D.3 DESCRIPTIVE STATISTICS

TABLE D.1 *Descriptive statistics for traders in markets on local government and private land.*

Statistic	N	Mean	St. Dev.	Min	Max	Local govt. land	Private land	p-value
Represent	670	0.63	0.35	0	1	0.71	0.61	0.002
Honest account	519	0.76	0.42	0	1	0.88	0.73	0.000
Free complain	674	0.92	0.27	0	1	0.92	0.92	0.927
Resolve disputes	699	0.37	0.48	0	1	0.42	0.36	0.189
Postsec. education	729	0.45	0.50	0	1	0.43	0.46	0.484
Men	729	0.74	0.44	0	1	0.67	0.76	0.047
Number employees	729	0.52	0.91	0	8	0.43	0.54	0.152
Annual rent (USD)	610	2,292.35	1,944.58	1.21	21,829.23	2004.00	2365.28	0.022
Stock value (USD)	469	15,018.86	26,770.38	251.26	301,507.50	15026.84	15017.01	0.998
Sell apparel	729	0.58	0.49	0	1	0.59	0.57	0.622
Sell electronics	729	0.16	0.36	0	1	0.08	0.18	0.000
Sell beauty	729	0.05	0.22	0	1	0.13	0.03	0.001
Sell hardware	729	0.09	0.29	0	1	0.05	0.10	0.019
Sell home goods	729	0.13	0.34	0	1	0.29	0.09	0.000
Leader for life	695	0.02	0.12	0	1	0.01	0.02	0.228
Leader provides political info	666	0.53	0.50	0	1	0.68	0.49	0.000
Sleep election eve	584	0.08	0.27	0	1	0.06	0.08	0.259

D.4 SOCIAL DESIRABILITY BIAS

A potential concern might be that traders are reluctant to speak openly about predatory leaders, especially if other individuals could hear their responses. I asked enumerators to report who else was present during the interview, and 33 percent said no one else was present. To assess whether I should be concerned about social desirability bias, I conducted a t-test comparing how traders respond when asked about their market association leader based on whether or not others were present during the interview. As shown in Table D.2, there does not appear to be cause for concern; there is no evidence traders are less critical when others are present, and indeed the opposite might even be the case.

TABLE D.2 *Average responses to questions about market leadership based on whether anyone else was present during the interview.*

	No one present	Others present	p-value
Represent	0.70	0.59	0.000
Honest accounting	0.77	0.76	0.895
Free to complain	0.95	0.90	0.022
Help to resolve disputes	0.40	0.36	0.287

TABLE D.3 *This table shows the results of t-tests that compare the proportion of traders selling in various product categories across market land type. (This table subsets the data to markets with data from five or more traders.)*

	Local government land	Private land	p-value
Proportion apparel	0.540	0.645	0.481
Proportion electronics	0.027	0.163	0.074
Proportion beauty	0.298	0.035	0.112
Proportion hardware	0.016	0.053	0.17
Proportion home	0.120	0.105	0.856

Appendix E

Appendix to Chapter 7 – Private Groups in Comparative Perspective

TABLE E.1 *This table shows the relationship between what traders report as the total value of stock in their shop and market good governance indicators, and land. Standard errors are clustered at the market association level.*

	Dependent variable				
	Represent (1)	Honest accounting (2)	Free to complain (3)	Resolve dispute (4)	Stock value (log) (5)
Stock value (log)	−0.01 (0.02)	−0.0004 (0.02)	−0.01 (0.01)	−0.04** (0.02)	
Local government land					−0.17 (0.21)
Constant	0.76*** (0.26)	0.79*** (0.27)	1.00*** (0.16)	0.94*** (0.25)	14.12*** (0.08)
Observations	438	344	442	455	467
Controls	No	No	No	No	No
LGA fixed effects	No	No	No	No	No

Note: *p<0.1; **p<0.05; ***p<0.01

Bibliography

Acemoglu, Daron, Tristan Reed and James A. Robinson. 2014. "Chiefs: Economic development and elite control of civil society in Sierra Leone." *Journal of Political Economy* 122(2):319–368.

Auerbach, Adam M. 2016. "Clients and communities: The political economy of party network organization and development in India's urban slums." *World Politics* 68(1):111–148.

Auerbach, Adam M. 2017. "Neighborhood associations and the urban poor: India's Slum Development Committees." *World Development* 96:119–135.

Auerbach, Adam M., Adrienne LeBas, Alison E. Post and Rebecca Weitz-Shapiro. 2018. "State, society, and informality in cities of the Global South." *Studies in Comparative International Development* 53(3):261–280.

Auerbach, Adam and Tariq Thachil. 2018. "How clients select brokers: Competition and choice in India's slums." *American Political Science Review* 112(4):775–791.

Awam, James. 2014. *Heirs of a heritage: Unconventional leadership strategies in Lagos.* The James & Solomons Company.

Barkan, Joel D., Alex Gboyega and Mike Stevens. 2002. "State and local governance in Nigeria." *World Bank Report*, http://documents1.worldbank.org/curated/en/442501468780898611/pdf/multipage.pdf.

Barnes, Nicholas. 2017. Monopolies of violence: Criminal governance in Rio de Janeiro PhD thesis University of Wisconsin – Madison.

Bates, Robert H. 1988. "Contra contractarianism: Some reflections on the new institutionalism." *Politics and Society* 16(2–3):387–401.

Bates, Robert H. and Da-Hsiang Donald Lien. 1985. "A note on taxation, development, and representative government." *Politics and Society* 14(1):53–70.

Beck, Thorsten and Robert Cull. 2014. Small and Medium-Sized Enterprise Finance in Africa. Technical report Africa Growth Initiative at Brookings, www.brookings.edu/wp-content/uploads/2016/06/SME-Finance-in-Africa-Designed_FINAL.pdf.

Berman, Sheri. 1997. "Civil society and the collapse of the Weimar Republic." *World Politics* 49(3):401–429.

Bernstein, Lisa. 1992. "Opting out of the legal system: Extralegal contractual relations in the diamond industry." *The Journal of Legal Studies* 21(1):115–157.

Bernstein, Lisa. 2001. "Private commercial law in the cotton industry: Creating cooperation through rules, norms, and institutions." *Michigan Law Review* 99(7):1724–1790.

Biggs, Tyler and Manju Kedia Shah. 2006. "African small and medium enterprises, networks, and manufacturing performance." *World Bank Policy Research Working paper 3855*, https://openknowledge.worldbank.org/handle/10986/8752.

Brady, Henry E. and David Collier. 2010. *Rethinking social inquiry: Diverse tools, shared standards*. Rowman & Littlefield Publishers.

Brigham, John. 1993. "Order without lawyers: Ellickson on how neighbors settle disputes." *Law & Society Review*, 27(3):609–618.

Cai, Jing and Adam Szeidl. 2017. "Interfirm relationships and business performance." *The Quarterly Journal of Economics* 133(3):1229–1282.

Centeno, Miguel Angel. 2003. *Blood and debt: War and the nation-state in Latin America*. Penn State Press.

Cervero, Rober and Aaron Golub. 2011. "Informal public transport: A global perspective." In *Urban transport in the developing world: A handbook of policy and practice*, ed. Harry T. Dimitriou and Ralph Gakenheimer. Cheltenham: Edward Elgar.

Cross, John Christopher. 1998. *Informal politics: Street vendors and the state in Mexico City*. Stanford University Press.

de Gramont, Diane. 2014. *Constructing the Megacity: The dynamics of state-building in Lagos, Nigeria, 1999–2013*. Unpublished masters thesis.

De Mel, Suresh, David McKenzie and Christopher Woodruff. 2008. "Returns to capital in microenterprises: Evidence from a field experiment." *The Quarterly Journal of Economics* 123(4):1329–1372.

Dixit, Avinash K. 2004. *Lawlessness and economics: Alternative modes of governance*. Princeton University Press.

Doner, Richard F. 1992. "Limits of state strength: Toward an institutionalist view of economic development." *World Politics* 44(3):398–431.

Duggan, Catherine. Forthcoming. *The institutional foundations of lending: Indirect regulation and state-building*. Cambridge University Press.

Easterly, William and Ross Levine. 1997. "Africa's growth tragedy: Policies and ethnic divisions." *The Quarterly Journal of Economics* 112(4):1203–1250.

Ellickson, Robert. 1991. *Order without law: How neighbors settle disputes*. Harvard University Press.

Evans, Peter B. 1995. *Embedded autonomy: States and industrial transformation*. Cambridge University Press.

Fearon, James D. and David D. Laitin. 1996. "Explaining interethnic cooperation." *American Political Science Review*, 90(4):715–735.

Frye, Timothy. 2000. *Brokers and bureaucrats: Building market institutions in Russia*. University of Michigan Press.

Gay, Robert. 2010. *Popular organization and democracy in Rio de Janeiro: A tale of two favelas*. Temple University Press.

Ghandchi-Tehrani, Davoud. 1983. "Bazaaris and Clergy: Socio-economic origins of radicalism and revolution in Iran." Ph.D. dissertation, City University of New York.

Ghemawat, Pankaj and Tarun Khanna. 1998. "The nature of diversified business groups: A research design and two case studies." *The Journal of Industrial Economics* 46(1):35–61.

Gibbons, Robert and Rebecca Henderson. 2012. "Relational contracts and organizational capabilities." *Organization Science* 23(5):1350–1364.

Goertz, Gary and James Mahoney. 2012. *A tale of two cultures: Qualitative and quantitative research in the social sciences*. Princeton University Press.

Goodfellow, Tom. 2015. "Taming the 'Rogue' sector: Studying state effectiveness in Africa through informal transport politics." *Comparative Politics* 47(2):127–147.

Goodfellow, Tom. 2016. "'Double capture' and de-democratisation: Interest group politics and Uganda's 'transport mafia'." *The Journal of Development Studies*, 53(10):1–16.

Granovetter, Mark. 1985. "Economic action and social structure: The problem of embeddedness." *American Journal of Sociology*, 91(5):481–510.

Greif, Avner. 1993. "Contract enforceability and economic institutions in early trade: The Maghribi traders' coalition." *The American Economic Review* 83(3): 525–548.

Greif, Avner. 2006. *Institutions and the path to the modern economy*. Cambridge University Press.

Grossman, Shelby. 2020. "The politics of order in informal markets: Evidence from Lagos." *World Politics* 72(1):47–79.

Habyarimana, James P. 2009. *Coethnicity: Diversity and the dilemmas of collective action*. Russell Sage Foundation.

Hadfield, Gillian K. and Barry R. Weingast. 2013. "Law without the state: Legal attributes and the coordination of decentralized collective punishment." *Journal of Law and Courts* 1(1):3–34.

Hadfield, Gillian K. and Barry R. Weingast. 2014. "Microfoundations of the rule of law." *Annual Review of Political Science* 17:21–42.

Hardy, Morgan and Jamie McCasland. 2016. "It takes two: Experimental evidence on the determinants of technology diffusion." *Unpublished paper, University of British Columbia*.

Holland, Alisha C. 2015. "The distributive politics of enforcement." *American Journal of Political Science* 59(2):357–371.

Holland, Alisha C. 2016. "Forbearance." *American Political Science Review* 110(2):232–246.

Hummel, Calla. 2017*a*. "Disobedient markets: Street vendors, enforcement, and state intervention in collective action." *Comparative Political Studies*, 50(11): https://doi.org/10.1177/0010414016679177.

Hummel, Calla. 2017*b*. Disobedient markets: Street vendors, enforcement, and state intervention in collective action PhD thesis The University of Texas at Austin.

Ingleby, Richard. 1994. "Robert C. Ellickson, order without law: How neighbors settle disputes." *The Modern Law Review* 57(2):330–331.

Ivaldi, Marc, Bruno Jullien, Patrick Rey, Paul Seabright and Jean Tirole. 2007. "The economics of tacit collusion: Implications for merger control." In *The Political Economy of Antitrust*, ed. Vivek Ghosal and Johan Stennek. Amsterdam, The Netherlands: Elsevier.

Johnson, Cheryl Jeffries. 1978. Nigerian women and British colonialism: The Yoruba example with selected biographies PhD thesis Northwestern University.

Johnson, Cheryl P. 1982. "Grassroots organizing: Women in anticolonial activity in Southwestern Nigeria." *African Studies Review* 25(2–3):137–157.

Kang, David C. 2002. *Crony capitalism: Corruption and development in South Korea and the Philippines*. Cambridge University Press.

Keshavarzian, Arang. 2007. *Bazaar and state in Iran: The politics of the Tehran marketplace*. Vol. 26 Cambridge University Press.

King, Andrew A. and Michael J. Lenox. 2000. "Industry self-regulation without sanctions: The chemical industry's responsible care program." *Academy of Management Journal* 43(4):698–716.

Klein, Benjamin and Keith B. Leffler. 1981. "The role of market forces in assuring contractual performance." *Journal of Political Economy* 89(4):615–641.

Kok, Jan de and Mario Berrios. 2019. "Small matters: Global evidence on the contribution to employment by the self-employed, micro-enterprises and SMEs." www.ilo.org/wcmsp5/groups/public/—dgreports/—dcomm/—publ/documents/publication/wcms_723282.pdf.

Lagos Statistics Bureau. 2012. "2012 Lagos state household survey."

Larson, Jennifer M. 2017. "Networks and interethnic cooperation." *The Journal of Politics* 79(2):546–559.

Lawanson, Taibat. 2014. "Illegal urban entrepreneurship? The case of street vendors in Lagos, Nigeria." *Journal of Architecture & Environment*, 13(1):45–60.

Leeson, Peter T. 2007. "An-arrgh-chy: The law and economics of pirate organization." *Journal of Political Economy* 115(6):1049–1094.

Leeson, Peter T. 2014. *Anarchy unbound: Why self-governance works better than you think*. Cambridge University Press.

Leff, Nathaniel H. 1978. "Industrial organization and entrepreneurship in the developing countries: The economic groups." *Economic Development and Cultural Change* 26(4):661–675.

Leke, Acha, Reinaldo Fiorini, Richard Dobbs, Fraser Thompson, Aliyu Suleiman and David Wright. 2014. "Nigeria's renewal: Delivering inclusive growth." *McKinsey Global Institute Insight and Publications*, www.mckinsey.com/~/media/McKinsey/Featured%20Insights/Middle%20East%20and%20Africa/Nigerias%20renewal%20Delivering%20inclusive%20growth/MGI_Nigerias_renewal_Full_report.pdf.

Luong, Pauline Jones and Erika Weinthal. 2004. "Contra coercion: Russian tax reform, exogenous shocks, and negotiated institutional change." *American Political Science Review* 98(1):139–152.

Macneil, Ian R. 1977. "Contracts: Adjustment of long-term economic relations under classical, neoclassical, and relational contract law." *Northwestern University Law Review* 72:854.

Markus, Stanislav. 2012. "Secure property as a bottom-up process: Firms, stakeholders, and predators in weak states." *World Politics* 64(2):242–277.

Marshall, Robert C. and Leslie M. Marx. 2012. *The economics of collusion: Cartels and bidding rings*. Mit Press.

Mattingly, Daniel C. 2016. "Elite capture." *World Politics* 68(3):383–412.

Maxfield, Sylvia and Ben Ross Schneider. 1997. *Business and the state in developing countries*. Cornell University Press.

McKenzie, David and Christopher Woodruff. 2008. "Experimental evidence on returns to capital and access to finance in Mexico." *The World Bank Economic Review* 22(3):457–482.

McMillan, J. and C. Woodruff. 1999. "Dispute prevention without courts in Vietnam." *Journal of Law, Economics, and Organization* 15(3):637–658.

McMillan, John and Christopher Woodruff. 2000. "Private order under dysfunctional public order." *Michigan Law Review*, 98(8):2421–2458.

McPherson, Michael A. 1996. "Growth of micro and small enterprises in southern Africa." *Journal of Development Economics* 48(2):253–277.

Mead, Donald C. and Carl Liedholm. 1998. "The dynamics of micro and small enterprises in developing countries." *World Development* 26(1):61–74.

Miguel, Edward and Mary Kay Gugerty. 2005. "Ethnic diversity, social sanctions, and public goods in Kenya." *Journal of Public Economics* 89(11):2325–2368.

Milgrom, Paul, Douglass North and Barry Weingast. 1990. "The role of institutions in the revival of trade: The Law Merchant, private judges, and the Champagne Fairs." *Economics and Politics* 2(1):1–23.

Milner, Helen V. and Nita Rudra. 2015. "Globalization and the political benefits of the informal economy." *International Studies Review* 17(4):664–669.

Mitlin, Diana. 2008. "With and beyond the state: Co-production as a route to political influence, power and transformation for grassroots organizations." *Environment and Urbanization* 20(2):339–360.

Mozaffari, Mehdi. 1991. "Why the bazar rebels." *Journal of Peace Research* 28(4):377–391.

Murtazashvili, Ilia. 2013. *The political economy of the American frontier.* Cambridge University Press.

Nash, Jennifer and John Ehrenfeld. 1997. "Codes of environmental management practice: Assessing their potential as a tool for change." *Annual Review of Energy and the Environment* 22(1):487–535.

Nathan, Noah L. 2016. "Local ethnic geography, expectations of favoritism, and voting in urban Ghana." *Comparative Political Studies* 49(14):1896–1929.

North, Douglass C. 1993. "Institutions and credible commitment." *Journal of Institutional and Theoretical Economics (JITE)/Zeitschrift für die gesamte Staatswissenschaft,* 149(1):11–23.

North, Douglass Cecil, John Joseph Wallis and Barry R. Weingast. 2009. *Violence and social orders: A conceptual framework for interpreting recorded human history.* Taylor & Francis.

Office of State Auditor General. 2012. "2012 Audit report of Local Government and Local Council Development Areas in Lagos State."

Ogilvie, Sheilagh. 2004. "Guilds, efficiency, and social capital: evidence from German proto-industry." *Economic History Review,* 57(2):286–333.

Ogilvie, Sheilagh. 2014. "The economics of guilds." *The Journal of Economic Perspectives,* 28(4):169–192.

Olson, Mancur. 1965. *The logic of collective action: Public goods and the theory of group.* Harvard University Press Cambridge.

Olson, Mancur. 1993. "Dictatorship, democracy, and development." *American Political Science Review* 87(3):567–576.

Olson, Mancur. 2000. *Power and prosperity: Outgrowing communist and capitalist dictatorships.* Basic Books.

Ostrom, Elinor. 1990. *Governing the commons: The evolution of institutions for collective action.* Cambridge University Press.

Ostrom, Elinor. 1996. "Crossing the great divide: Coproduction, synergy, and development." *World Development* 24(6):1073–1087.

Ostrom, Elinor. 2005. "Self-governance and forest resources." *Terracotta reader: A market approach to the environment. Academic Foundation, New Delhi* pp. 131–155.

Owen, Olly. 2017. "Risk and motivation in police work in Nigeria." In *Police in Africa: The street level view,* ed. Jan Beek, Mirco Göpfert, Olly Owen and Johnny Steinberg. Oxford University Press.

Oyemakinde, Wale. 1973. "The Pullen marketing scheme: A trial in food price control in Nigeria, 1941–1947." *Journal of the Historical Society of Nigeria,* 6(4):413–423.

Padilla, A. Jorge and Marco Pagano. 1997. "Endogenous communication among lenders and entrepreneurial incentives." *The Review of Financial Studies* 10(1):205–236.

Paller, Jeffrey. 2019. *Democracy in Ghana: Everyday politics in urban Africa.* Cambridge University Press.

Paller, Jeffrey W. 2015. "Informal networks and access to power to obtain housing in urban slums in Ghana." *Africa Today* 62(1):30–55.

Park, Seung Ho and Michael V. Russo. 1996. "When competition eclipses cooperation: An event history analysis of joint venture failure." *Management Science* 42(6):875–890.

Parsa, Misagh. 1989. *Social origins of the Iranian revolution.* Rutgers University Press.

Polanyi, Karl. 1944. *The great transformation: The political and economic origins of our time.* Beacon Press.

Post, Alison E. 2014. *Foreign and domestic investment in Argentina: the politics of privatized infrastructure.* Cambridge University Press.

Post, Alison E. 2018. "Cities and politics in the developing world." *Annual Review of Political Science* 21:115–133.

Rapson, R. N. 1959. Report of an Inquiry by Mr. R. N. Rapson, M.V.O., into alleged irregularities by the Lagos Town Council in connection with the collection of money and the issue of permits and the allocation of market stalls in respect of proposed temporary markets at Ereko and Oko-Awo. Technical report Federation of Nigeria.

Richman, Barak D. 2004. "Firms, courts, and reputation mechanisms: towards a positive theory of private ordering." *Columbia Law Review* 104:2328.

Richman, Barak D. 2006. "How community institutions create economic advantage: Jewish diamond merchants in New York." *Law & Social Inquiry* 31(2):383–420.

Richman, Barak D. 2017. *Stateless Commerce: The Diamond Network and the Persistence of Relational Exchange.* Harvard University Press.

Robinson, Amanda. 2016. "Internal borders: Ethnic-based market segmentation in Malawi." *World Development* 87:371–384.

Schmitz, Hubert and Khalid Nadvi. 1999. "Clustering and industrialization: introduction." *World Development* 27(9):1503–1514.

Schneider, Friedrich. 2005. "Shadow economies around the world: What do we really know?" *European Journal of Political Economy* 21(3):598–642.

Skarbek, David. 2014. *The social order of the underworld: How prison gangs govern the American penal system.* Oxford University Press.

Sklar, Richard L. 2004. *Nigerian political parties: Power in an emergent African nation.* Africa World Press.

Startz, Meredith. 2018. "The value of face-to-face: Search and contracting problems in Nigerian trade." *Working Paper,* https://sites.google.com/site/meredithstartz/research.

Stringham, Edward. 2003. "The extralegal development of securities trading in seventeenth-century Amsterdam." *The Quarterly Review of Economics and Finance* 43(2):321–344.

Stringham, Edward Peter. 2002. "The emergence of the London stock exchange as a self-policing club." *Journal of Private Enterprise* 17(2):1–19.

Stringham, Edward Peter. 2015. *Private governance: Creating order in economic and social life.* Oxford University Press.

Szwarcberg, Mariela. 2015. *Mobilizing poor voters: Machine politics, clientelism, and social networks in Argentina.* Cambridge University Press.

Thachil, Tariq. 2015. "Does police repression increase cooperation between migrants? A study of informal urban marketplaces in India." *A Study of Informal Urban Marketplaces in India (August 13, 2015)*.

Thachil, Tariq. 2017. "Do rural migrants divide ethnically in the city? Evidence from an ethnographic experiment in India." *American Journal of Political Science* 61(4):908–926.

Thachil, Tariq. 2018. "Improving surveys through ethnography: Insights from India's urban periphery." *Forthcoming at Studies in Comparative International Development*.

Tilly, Charles. 1992. *Coercion, capital, and European states, AD 990–1992*. Blackwell Oxford.

Tsai, Lily L. 2007. *Accountability without democracy: Solidary groups and public goods provision in rural China*. Cambridge University Press.

Uzzi, Brian. 1996. "The sources and consequences of embeddedness for the economic performance of organizations: The network effect." *American Sociological Review*, 61(4):674–698.

Weingast, Barry R. 1995. "The economic role of political institutions: Market-preserving federalism and economic development." *Journal of Law, Economics, & Organization*, 11(1):1–31.

Williams, Colin C. and Muhammad S. Shahid. 2016. "Informal entrepreneurship and institutional theory: explaining the varying degrees of (in) formalization of entrepreneurs in Pakistan." *Entrepreneurship & Regional Development* 28(1–2): 1–25.

Williamson, Oliver E. 1971. "The vertical integration of production: Market failure considerations." *The American Economic Review* 61(2):112–123.

Williamson, Oliver E. 1983. "Credible commitments: Using hostages to support exchange." *The American Economic Review*, 73(4):519–540.

World Bank. 2007. "World bank enterprise surveys."

World Bank. 2009. "Sample survey methodology design for enterprise survey (Productivity and Investment Climate Survey) in Nigeria."

World Bank. 2010. "Guatemala enterprise informal survey implementation note."

World Bank. 2014. "Doing business 2015: Going beyond efficiency."

World urbanization prospects the 2014 revision. 2015. *United Nations, Department of Economic and Social Affairs*.

Index

Lightning Source UK Ltd.
Milton Keynes UK
UKHW021834081222
413600UK00014B/374